Forgotten Books

The Hittites the Story of a Forgotten Empire

By

A. H. Sayce

Published by Forgotten Books 2012

PIBN 1000288691

By-Paths of Bible Knowledge

XII

THE HITTITES

THE STORY OF A FORGOTTEN EMPIRE

BY

A. H. SAYCE, LL.D.

PROFESSOR OF ASSYRIOLOGY, OXFORD

AUTHOR OF 'FRESH LIGHT FROM THE ANCIENT MONUMENTS'

'ASSYRIA, ITS PRINCES, PRIESTS, AND PEOPLE,' ETC. ETC.

SECOND EDITION

FLEMING H. REVELL COMPANY

NEW YORK | CHICAGO

112 FIFTH AVENUE | 148 & 150 MADISON STREET

The Religious Tract Society, London

PREFACE.

THE discovery of the important place once occupied by the Hittites has been termed 'the romance of ancient history.' Nothing can be more interesting than the resurrection of a forgotten people, more especially when that people is so intimately connected with Old Testament story, and with the fortunes of the Chosen Race. How the resurrection has been accomplished, by putting together the fragmentary evidence of Egyptian and Assyrian inscriptions, of strange-looking monuments in Asia Minor, and of still undeciphered hieroglyphics, will be described in the following pages. It is marvellous to think that only ten years ago 'the romance' could not have been written, and that the part played by the Hittite nations in the history of the world was still unsuspected. Yet now we have become, as it were, familiar with the friends of Abraham and the race to which Uriah belonged.

Already a large and increasing literature has been devoted to them. The foundation stone, which was laid by my paper 'On the Monuments of the Hittites' in 1880, has been crowned with a stately edifice in Dr. Wright's *Empire of the Hittites*, of which the second edition appeared in 1886, and in the fourth volume of the magnificent work of Prof. Perrot and

M. Chipiez, *L'Histoire de l'Art dans l'Antiquite*, published at Paris a year ago. Profusely illustrated, the latter work sets before us a life-like picture of Hittite architecture and art.

It cannot be long before the inscriptions left to us by the Hittites, in their peculiar form of hieroglyphic writing, are also made to reveal their secrets. All that is required are more materials upon which to work, and we shall then know which, if any, of the attempts hitherto made to explain them has hit the truth. Major Conder's system of decipherment has not yet obtained the adhesion of other scholars ; neither has the rival system of Mr. Ball, ingenious and learned as it is. But if we may judge from the successes of the last few years, it cannot be long before we know as much about the Hittite language and writing as we now know about Hittite art and civilisation. To quote the words of Dr. Wright : 'We must labour to unloose the dumb tongue of these inscriptions, and to unlock their mysteries, not with the view of finding something sensational in them, or for the purpose of advancing some theory, but for the love of knowing what they really contain ; and I doubt not that, proceeding in the right method of investigation, we shall reach results satisfactory to the Oriental scholar, and confirmatory of Divine truth.'

A. H. SAYCE.

QUEEN'S COLLEGE, OXFORD.
October 1888.

TABLE OF CONTENTS.

—◆◆—

LIST OF ILLUSTRATIONS.

———◆◆———

MAP ILLUSTRATING THE EXTENT OF THE HITTITE EMPIRE.

(*Copied by permission from ‘ The Empire of the Hittites.*)

THE HITTITES

THE STORY OF A FORGOTTEN EMPIRE.

CHAPTER I.

THE HITTITES OF THE BIBLE.

E are told in the Second Book of Kings (vii. 6) that
when the Syrians were encamped about Samaria
and the Lord had sent a panic upon them, 'they said
one to another, Lo, the king of Israel hath hired against
us the kings of the Hittites, and the kings of the
Egyptians, to come upon us.' Nearly forty years ago
a distinguished scholar selected this passage for his
criticism. Its 'unhistorical tone,' he declared, 'is too
manifest to allow of our easy belief in it.' 'No Hittite
kings can have compared in power with the king of
Judah, the real and near ally, who is not named at
all ... nor is there a single mark of acquaintance with
the contemporaneous history.'

Recent discoveries have retorted the critic's objections
upon himself. It is not the Biblical writer but the
modern author who is now proved to have been un-
acquainted with the contemporaneous history of the
time. The Hittites were a very real power. Not very
many centuries before the age of Elisha they had
contested the empire of Western Asia with the Egyptians,
and though their power had waned in the days of

Jehoram they were still formidable enemies and useful allies. They were still worthy of comparison with the divided kingdom of Egypt, and infinitely more powerful than that of Judah.

But we hear no more about them in the subsequent records of the Old Testament. The age of Hittite supremacy belongs to an earlier date than the rise of the monarchy in Israel ; earlier, we may even say, than the Israelitish conquest of Canaan. The references to them in the later historical books of the Old Testament Canon are rare and scanty. The traitor who handed over Beth-el to the house of Joseph fled 'into the land of the Hittites' (Judg. i. 26), and there built a city which he called Luz. Mr. Tomkins thinks he has found it in the town of Latsa, captured by the Egyptian king Ramses II., which he identifies with Qalb Luzeh, in Northern Syria. However this may be, an emended reading of the text, based upon the Septuagint, transforms the unintelligible Tahtim-hodshi of 2 Sam. xxiv. 6 into 'the Hittites of Kadesh,' a city which long continued to be their chief stronghold in the valley of the Orontes. It was as far as this city, which lay at 'the entering in of Hamath,' on the northern frontier of the Israelitish kingdom, that the officers of David made their way when they were sent to number Israel. Lastly, in the reign of Solomon the Hittites are again mentioned (1 Kings x. 28, 29) in a passage where the authorised translation has obscured the sense. It runs in the Revised Version : ' And the horses which Solomon had were brought out of Egypt ; and the king's merchants received them in droves, each drove at a price. And a chariot came up and went out of Egypt for six hundred shekels of silver, and an horse for an hundred and fifty: and so for all the kings of the Hittites, and for the kings of Syria, did they bring them out by their means.' The Hebrew merchants, in fact, were the mediatories between Egypt and the north, and exported the horses of Egypt not only for the king of Israel but for the kings of the Hittites as well.

The Hittites whose cities and princes are thus referred to in the later historical books of the Old Testament belonged to the north, Hamath and Kadesh on the Orontes being their most southernly points. But the Book of Genesis introduces us to other Hittites—'the children of Heth,' as they are termed—whose seats were in the extreme south of Palestine. It was from 'Ephron the Hittite' that Abraham bought the cave of Machpelah at Hebron (Gen. xxiii.), and Esau 'took to wife Judith the daughter of Beeri the Hittite, and Bashemath the daughter of Elon the Hittite' (Gen. xxvi. 34), or, as it is given elsewhere, 'Adah the daughter of Elon the Hittite' (Gen. xxxvi. 2). It must be to these Hittites of the south that the ethnographical table in the tenth chapter of Genesis refers when it is said that 'Canaan begat Sidon his first-born, and Heth' (ver. 15), and in no other way can we explain the statement of Ezekiel (xvi. 3, 45) that 'the father' of Jerusalem 'was an Amorite and' its 'mother a Hittite.' 'Uriah the Hittite,' too, the trusty officer of David, must have come from the neighbourhood of Hebron, where David had reigned for seven years, rather than from among the distant Hittites of the north. Besides the latter there was thus a Hittite population which clustered round Hebron, and to whom the origin of Jerusalem was partly due.

Now it will be noticed that the prophet ascribes the foundation of Jerusalem to the Amorite as well as the Hittite. The Jebusites, accordingly, from whose hands the city was wrested by David, must have belonged to one or other of these two great races; perhaps, indeed, to both. At all events, we find elsewhere that the Hittites and Amorites are closely interlocked together. It was so at Hebron, where in the time of Abraham not only Ephron the Hittite dwelt, but also the three sons of the Amorite Mamre (Gen. xiv. 13). The Egyptian monuments show that the two nations were similarly confederated together at Kadesh on the Orontes. Kadesh was a Hittite stronghold; nevertheless it is described as being 'in the land of the Amaur' or Amorites, and its king is depicted with the physical characteristics of the Amorite, and not of the Hittite. Further north, in the country which the Hittites had made peculiarly their own, cities existed which bore names, it would seem, compounded with that of the Amorite, and the common Assyrian title of the district in which Damascus stood, Gar-emeris, is best explained as 'the *Gar* of the Amorites.' Shechem was taken by Jacob 'out of the hand of the Amorite' (Gen. xlviii. 22), and the Amorite kingdom of Og and Sihon included large tracts on the eastern side of the Jordan. South of Palestine the block of mountains in which the sanctuary of Kadesh-barnea stood was an Amorite possession (Gen. xiv. 7, Deut. i. 19, 20); and we learn from Numb. xiii. 29, that while the Amalekites dwelt 'in the land of the south' and the Canaanites by the sea and in the valley of the Jordan, the Hittites and Jebusites and Amorites lived together in the mountains of the interior. Among the five kings of the Amorites against whom Joshua fought (Josh. x. 5) were the king of Jerusalem and the king of Hebron.

The Hittites and Amorites were therefore mingled together in the mountains of Palestine like the two races which ethnologists tell us go to form the modern Kelt. But the Egyptian monuments teach us that they were of very different.origin and character. The Hittites were a people with yellow skins and 'Mongoloid' features, whose receding foreheads, oblique eyes, and protruding upper jaws, are represented as faithfully on their own monuments as they are on those of Egypt, so that we cannot accuse the Egyptian artists of caricaturing their enemies. If the Egyptians have made the Hittites ugly, it was because they were so in reality. The Amorites, on the contrary, were a tall and handsome people. They are depicted with white skins, blue eyes, and reddish hair, all the characteristics, in fact, of the white race. Mr. Petrie points out their resemblance to the Dardanians of Asia Minor, who form an intermediate link between the white-skinned tribes of the Greek seas and the fair-complexioned Libyans of Northern Africa. The latter are stil! found in large numbers in the mountainous regions which stretch eastward from Morocco, and are usually known among the French under the name of Kabyles. The traveller who first meets with them in Algeria cannot fail to be struck by their likeness to a certain part of the population in the British Isles. Their clear-white freckled skins, their blue eyes, their golden-red hair and tall stature, remind him of the fair Kelts of an Irish village ; and when we find that their skulls, which are of the so-called dolichocephalic or 'long-headed' type, are the same as the skulls discovered in the prehistoric cromlechs of the country they still inhabit, we may conclude that they represent the modern descendants of the white-skinned Libyans of the Egyptian monuments.

In Palestine also we still come across representatives of a fair-complexioned blue-eyed race, in whom we may see the descendants of the ancient Amorites, just as we see in the Kabyles the descendants of the ancient Libyans. We know that the Amorite type continued to exist in Judah long after the Israelitish conquest of Canaan. The captives taken from the southern cities of Judah by Shishak in the time of Rehoboam, and depicted by him upon the walls of the great temple of Karnak, are people of Amorite origin. Their 'regular profile of sub-aquiline cast,' as Mr. Tomkins describes it, their high cheek-bones and martial expression, are the features of the Amorites, and not of the Jews.

Tallness of stature has always been a distinguishing characteristic of the white race. Hence it was that the Anakim, the Amorite inhabitants of Hebron, seemed to the Hebrew spies to be as giants, while they themselves were but 'as grasshoppers' by the side of them (Numb. xiii. 33). After the Israelitish invasion remnants of the Anakim were left in Gaza and Gath and Ashkelon (Josh. xi. 22), and in the time of David Goliath of Gath and his gigantic family were objects of dread to their neighbours (2 Sam. xxi. 15–22).

It is clear, then, that the Amorites of Canaan belonged to the same white race as the Libyans of Northern Africa, and like them preferred the mountains to the hot plains and valleys below. The Libyans themselves belonged to a race which can be traced through the peninsula of Spain and the western side of France into the British Isles. Now it is curious that wherever this particular branch of the white race has extended it has been accompanied by a particular form of cromlech, or sepulchral chamber built of large uncut stones. The stones are placed upright in the ground and covered over with other large slabs, the whole chamber being subsequently concealed under a tumulus of small stones or earth. Not unfrequently the entrance to the crom-lech is approached by a sort of corridor. These crom-lechs are found in Britain, in France, in Spain, in Northern Africa, and in Palestine, more especially on the eastern side of the Jordan, and the skulls that have been exhumed from them are the skulls of men of the dolichocephalic or long-headed type.

It has been necessary to enter at this length into what has been discovered concerning the Amorites by recent research, in order to show how carefully they should be distinguished from the Hittites with whom they afterwards intermingled. They must have been in pos-session of Palestine long before the Hittites arrived there. They extended over a much wider area, since there are no traces of the Hittites at Shechem or on the eastern side of the Jordan, where the Amorites estab-lished two powerful kingdoms ; while the earliest mention of the Amorites in the Bible (Gen. xiv. 7) describes them as dwelling at Hazezon-tamar, or En-gedi, on the shores of the Dead Sea, where no Hittites are ever known to have settled. The Hittite colony in Palestine, moreover, was confined to a small district in the moun-tains of Judah : their strength lay far away in the north, where the Amorites were comparatively weak. It is true that Kadesh on the Orontes was in the hands of the Hittites ; but it is also true that it was ' in the land of the Amorites,' and this implies that they were its original occupants. We must regard the Amorites as the earlier population, among a part of whom the Hittites in later days settled and intermarried. At what epoch that event took place we are still unable to say.

CHAPTER II.

THE HITTITES ON THE MONUMENTS OF EGYPT AND ASSYRIA.

IN the preceding chapter we have seen what the Bible has to tell us about 'the children of Heth.' They were an important people in the north of Syria who were ruled by 'kings' in the days of Solomon, and whose power was formidable to their Syrian neighbours. But there was also a branch of them established in the extreme south of Palestine, where they inhabited the mountains along with the Amorites, and had taken a share in the foundation of Jerusalem. It was from one of the latter, Ephron the son of Zohar, that Abraham had purchased the cave of Machpelah at Hebron ; and one of the wives of Esau was of Hittite descent. In later times Uriah the Hittite was one of the chief officers of David, and his wife Bath-sheba was not only the mother of Solomon, but also the distant ancestress of Christ. For us, therefore, these Hittites of Judæa have a very special and peculiar interest.

The decipherment of the inscriptions of Egypt and Assyria has thrown a new light upon their origin and history, and shown that the race to which they belonged once played a leading part in the history of the civilised East. On the Egyptian monuments they are called Kheta (or better Khata), on those of Assyria Khatta or Khate, both words being exact equivalents of the Hebrew Kheth and Khitti.

The Kheta or Hittites first appear upon the scene

in the time of the Eighteenth Egyptian Dynasty. The foreign rule of the Hyksos or Shepherd princes had been overthrown, Egypt had recovered its independence, and its kings determined to retaliate upon Asia the sufferings brought upon their own country by the Asiatic invader. The war, which commenced with driving the Asiatic out of the Delta, ended by attacking him in his own lands of Palestine and Syria. Thothmes I. (about B.C. 1600) marched to the banks of the Euphrates and set up 'the boundary of the empire' in the country of Naharina. Naharina was the Biblical Aram Naharaim or 'Syria of the two rivers,' better known, perhaps, as Mesopotamia, and its situation has been ascertained by recent discoveries. It was the district called Mitanni by the Assyrians, who describe it as being 'in front of the land of the Hittites,' on the eastern bank of the Euphrates, between Carchemish and the mouth of the river Balikh. In the age of Thothmes I., it was the leading state in Western Asia. The Hittites had not as yet made themselves formidable, and the most dangerous enemy the Egyptian monarch was called upon to face were the people over whom Chushan-risha-thaim was king in later days (Judg. iii. 8). It is not until the reign of his son, Thothmes III., that the Hittites come to the front. They are distinguished as 'Great' and 'Little,' the latter name perhaps denoting the Hittites of the south of Judah. However this may be, Thothmes received tribute from 'the king of the great land of the Kheta,' which consisted of gold, negro-slaves, men-servants and maid-servants, oxen and servants. Whether the Hittites were as yet in possession of Kadesh we do not know. If they were, they would have taken part in the struggle against the Egyptians which took place around the walls of Megiddo, and was decided in favour of Thothmes only after a long series of campaigns.

Before Thothmes died, he had made Egypt mistress of Palestine and Syria as far as the banks of the Euphrates and the land of Naharina. One of the bravest of his captains tells us on the walls of his tomb how he had captured prisoners in the neighbourhood of Aleppo, and had waded through the waters of the Euphrates when his master assaulted the mighty Hittite fortress of Carchemish. Kadesh on the Orontes had already fallen, and for a time all Western Asia did homage to the Egyptian monarch, even the king of Assyria sending him presents and courting, as it would seem, his alliance. The Egyptian empire touched the land of Naharina on the east and the 'great land of the Hittites' on the north.

But neighbours so powerful could not remain long at peace. A fragmentary inscription records that the first campaign of Thothmes IV., the grandson of Thothmes III., was directed against the Hittites, and Amenophis III., the son and successor of Thothmes IV., found it necessary to support himself by entering into matrimonial alliance with the king of Naharina. The marriage had strange consequences for Egypt. The new queen brought with her not only a foreign name and foreign customs, but a foreign faith as well. She refused to worship Amun of Thebes and the other gods of Egypt, and clung to the religion of her fathers, whose supreme object of adoration was the solar disk. The Hittite monuments themselves bear witness to the prevalence of this worship in Northern Syria. The winged solar disk appears above the figure of a king which has been brought from Birejik on the Euphrates to the British Museum; and even at Boghaz Keui, far away in Northern Asia Minor, the winged solar disk has been carved by Hittite sculptors upon the rock.

Amenophis IV., the son of Amenophis III., was educated in the faith of his mother, and after his accession to the throne endeavoured to impose the new creed upon his unwilling subjects. The powerful priesthood of Thebes withstood him for a while, but at last he assumed the name of Khu-n-Aten. 'the refulgence of the solar disk,' and quitting Thebes and its ancient temples he built himself a new capital dedicated to the new divinity. It stood on the eastern bank of the Nile, to the north of Assiout, and its long line of ruins is now known to the natives under the name of Tel el-Amarna. The city was filled with the adherents of the new creed, and their tombs are yet to be found in the cliffs that enclose the desert on the east. Its existence, however, was of no long duration. After the death of Khu-n-Aten, 'the heretic king,' his throne was occupied by one or two princes who had embraced his faith; but their reigns were brief, and they were succeeded by a monarch who returned once more to the religion of his forefathers. The capital of Khu-n-Aten was deserted, and the objects found upon its site show that it was never again inhabited.

Among its ruins a discovery has recently been made which casts an unexpected light upon the history of the Oriental world in the century before the Exodus. A large collection of clay tablets has been found, similar to those disinterred from the mounds of Nineveh and Babylonia, and like the latter inscribed in cuneiform characters and in the Assyro-Babylonian language.

They consist for the most part of letters and despatches sent to Khu-n-Aten and his father, Amenophis III., by the governors and rulers of Palestine, Syria, Mesopotamia and Babylonia, and they prove that at that time Babylonian was the international language, and the complicated cuneiform system of writing the common means of intercourse, of the educated world. Many of them were transferred by Khu-n-Aten from the royal archives of Thebes to his new city at Tel el-Amarna ; the rest were received and stored up after the new city had been built. We learn from them that the Hittites were already pressing southward, and were causing serious alarm to the governors and allies of the Egyptian king. One of the tablets is a despatch from Northern Syria, praying the Egyptian monarch to send assistance against them as soon as possible.

The 'heresy' of Khu-n-Aten brought trouble and disunion into Egypt, and his immediate successors seem to have been forced to retire from Syria. So far from being able to aid their allies, the Egyptian generals found themselves no match for the Hittite armies. Ramses I., the founder of the Nineteenth Dynasty, was compelled to conclude a treaty, defensive and offensive, with the Hittite king Saplel, and thus to recognise that Hittite power was on an equality with that of Egypt.

From this time forward it becomes possible to speak of a Hittite empire. Kadesh was once more in Hittite hands, and the influence formerly enjoyed by Egypt in Palestine and Syria was now enjoyed by its rival. The rude mountaineers of the Taurus had descended into the fertile plains of the south, interrupting the intercourse between Babylonia and Canaan, and superseding the cuneiform characters of Chaldæa by their

own hieroglyphic writing. From henceforth the Babylonian language ceased to be the language of diplomacy
and education.

With Seti I., the son and successor of Ramses, the
power of Egypt again revived. He drove the Beduin
and other marauders across the frontiers of the desert
and pushed the war into Syria itself. The cities of the
Philistines again received Egyptian garrisons ; Seti
marched his armies as far as the Orontes, fell suddenly
upon Kadesh and took it by storm. The war was now
begun between Egypt and the Hittites, which lasted for
the next half-century. It left Egypt utterly exhausted,
and, in spite of the vainglorious boasts of its scribes
and poets, glad to make a peace which virtually handed
over to her rivals the possession of Asia Minor.

But at first success waited on the arms of Seti. He
led his armies once more to the Euphrates and the borders of Naharina, and compelled Mautal, the Hittite
monarch, to sue for peace. The natives of the Lebanon
received him with acclamations, and cut down their
cedars for his ships on the Nile.

When Seti died, however, the Hittites were again in
possession of Kadesh, and war had broken out between
them and his son Ramses II. The long reign of Ramses II. was a ceaseless struggle against his formidable
foes. The war was waged with varying success. Sometimes victory inclined to the Egyptians, sometimes to
their Hittite enemies. Its chief result was to bring
ruin and disaster upon the cities of the Canaanites.
Their land was devastated by the hostile armies which
traversed it ; their towns were sacked, now by the
Hittite invaders from the north, now by the soldiers
of Ramses from the south. It was little wonder that

their inhabitants fled to island fastnesses like Tyre, deserting the city on the mainland, which an Egyptian traveller of the age of Ramses tells us had been burnt not long before. We can understand now why they offered so slight a resistance to the invading Israelites. The Exodus took place shortly after the death of Ramses II., the Pharaoh of the oppression ; and when Joshua entered Palestine he found there a disunited people and a country exhausted by the long and terrible wars of the preceding century. The way had been prepared by the Hittites for the Israelitish conquest of Canaan.

Pentaur, a sort of Egyptian poet laureate, has left us an epic which records the heroic deeds of Ramses in his first campaign against the Hittites. The actual event which gave occasion to it was an act of bravery performed by the Egyptian monarch before the walls of Kadesh ; but the poet has transformed him into a hero capable of superhuman deeds, and has thus produced an epic poem which reminds us of the Greek Iliad. Its details, however, afford a welcome insight into the history of the time, and show to what a height of power the Hittite empire had advanced. Its king could summon to his aid vassal-allies not only from Syria, but from the distant regions of Asia Minor as well. The merchants of Carchemish, the islanders of Arvad, acknowledged his supremacy along with the Dardanians of the Troad and the Mæonians of Lydia. The Hittite empire was already a reality, extending from the banks of the Euphrates to the shores of the Ægean, and including both the cultured Semites of Syria and the rude barbarians of the Greek seas.

It was in the fifth year of the reign of Ramses (B. C.

1383) that the event occurred which was celebrated
by the Egyptian Homer. The Egyptian armies had
advanced to the Orontes and the neighbourhood of
Kadesh. There two Beduin spies were captured, who
averred that the Hittite king was far away in the north
with his forces, encamped at Aleppo. But the in-
telligence was false. The Hittites and their allies, multitudinous as the sand on the sea-shore, were really lying
in ambush hard by. In their train were the soldiers
of Naharina, of the Dardanians and of Mysia, along
with numberless other peoples who now owned the
Hittite sway. The Hittite monarch 'had left no people
on his road without bringing them with him. Their
number was endless; nothing like it had ever been
before. They covered mountains and valleys like
grasshoppers for their number. He had not left silver
or gold with his people; he had taken away all their
goods and possessions to give it to the people who
accompanied him to the war.'

The whole host was concealed in ambush on the
north-west side of Kadesh. Suddenly they arose and
fell upon the terrified Egyptians by the waters of the
Lake of the Amorites, the modern Lake of Homs.
The chariots and horses charged 'the legion of Ra-
Hormakhis,' and 'foot and horse gave way before them.'
The news was carried to the Pharaoh. 'He arose like
his father Month, he grasped his weapons, and put on
his armour like Baal.' His steed 'Victory in Thebes'
bore him in his chariot into the midst of the foe. Then
he looked behind him, and behold he was alone. The
bravest heroes of the Hittite host beset his retreat,
and 2500 hostile chariots were around him. He was
abandoned in the midst of the enemy: not a prince,

not a captain was with him. Then in his extreme
need the Pharaoh called upon his god Amun. 'Where
art thou, my father Amun? If this means that the
father has forgotten his son, have I done anything
without thy knowledge, or have I not gone and followed
the precepts of thy mouth? Never were the precepts
of thy mouth transgressed, nor have I broken thy commandments in any respect. Sovran lord of Egypt, who
makest the peoples that withstand thee to bow down,
what are these people of Asia to thy heart? Amun
brings them low who know not God. . . . Behold now,
Amun, I am in the midst of many unknown peoples
in great number. All have united themselves, and I am
all alone : no other is with me ; my warriors and my
charioteers have deserted me. I called to them, and
not one of them heard my voice.'

The petition of Ramses was heard. Amun 'reached
out his hand,' and declared that he was come to help
the Pharaoh against his foes. Then Ramses was
inspired with supernatural strength. 'I hurled,' he is
made to say, 'the dart with my right hand, I fought with
my left hand. I was like Baal in his hour before their
sight. I had found 2500 chariots ; I was in the midst
of them ; but they were dashed in pieces before my
horses.' The ground was covered with the slain, and the
Hittite king fled in terror. His princes again gathered
round the Pharaoh, and again Ramses scattered them
in a moment. Six times did he charge the Hittite host,
and six times they broke and were slaughtered. The
strength of Baal was 'in all the limbs' of the Egyptian
king.

Now at last his servants came to his aid. But the
victory had already been won, and all that remained

was for the Pharaoh to upbraid his army for their
cowardice and sloth. 'Have I not given what is good
to each of you,' he exclaims, 'that ye have left me, so
that I was alone in the midst of hostile hosts? For-
saken by you, my life was in peril, and you breathed
tranquilly, and I was alone. Could you not have said
in your hearts that I was a rampart of iron to you?'
It was the horses of the royal chariot and not the troops
who deserved reward, and who would obtain it when the
king arrived safely home. So Ramses 'returned in
victory and strength; he had smitten hundreds of
thousands all together in one place with his arm.'

At daybreak the following morning he desired to
renew the conflict. The serpent that glowed on the
front of his diadem 'spat fire' in the face of his
enemies. They were overawed by the deeds of valour
he had accomplished single-handed the day before, and
feared to resume the fight. 'They remained afar off,
and threw themselves down on the earth, to entreat the
king in the sight [of his army]. And the king had
power over them and slew them without their being
able to escape. As bodies tumbled before his horses,
so they lay there stretched out all together in their
blood. Then the king of the hostile people of the
Hittites sent a messenger to pray piteously to the great
name of the king, speaking thus: "Thou art Ra-Hor-
makhis. Thy terror is upon the land of the Hittites,
for thou hast broken the neck of the Hittites for ever
and ever." '

The army of Ramses seconded the prayer of the
herald that the Egyptians and Hittites should hence-
forward be 'brothers together.' A treaty was accordingly made; but it was soon broken, and it was not

until sixteen years later that peace was finally established between the two rival powers.

The act of personal prowess upon which the heroic poem of Pentaur was built may have covered what had really been a check to the Egyptian arms. At all events, it is significant that no attempt was made to capture Kadesh, and that even the poet acknowledges how ready the Egyptian soldiers were to come to terms with their enemies. Equally significant is the fact that the war against the Hittites still went on ; in the eighth year of the Pharaoh's reign Palestine was overrun and certain cities captured, including Dapur or Tabor 'in the land of the Amorites,' while other campaigns were directed against Ashkelon, in the south, and the city of Tunep or Tennib, in the north. When a lasting treaty of peace was at last concluded in the twenty-first year of Ramses, its conditions show that 'the great king of the Hittites' treated on equal terms with the great king of Egypt, and that even Ramses himself, whom later legend magnified into the Sesostris of the Greeks, was fain to acknowledge the power of his Hittite adversaries. The treaty was sealed by the marriage of the Pharaoh with the daughter of the Hittite king.

The treaty, of which we possess the Egyptian text in full, was a very remarkable one, not only because it is the first treaty of the kind of which we know, but also on account of its contents. It ran as follows [1] :—

'In the year twenty-one, in the month Tybi, on the 21st day of the month, in the reign of King Ramessu Miamun, the dispenser of life eternally and for ever, the worshipper of the divinities Amon-Ra (of Thebes),

---

[1] This translation is the one given by Brugsch in the second edition of the English translation of his *History of Egypt.*

Hormakhu (of Heliopolis), Ptah (of Memphis), Mut the lady of the Asher-lake (near Karnak), and Khonsu, the peace-loving, there took place a public sitting on the throne of Horus among the living, resembling his father Hormakhu in eternity, in eternity, evermore.

'On that day the king was in the city of Ramses, presenting his peace-offerings to his father Amon-Ra, and to the gods Hormakhu-Tum, to Ptah of Ramessu-Miamun, and to Sutekh, the strong, the son of the goddess of heaven Nut, that they might grant to him many thirty years' jubilee feasts, and innumerable happy years, and the subjection of all peoples under his feet for ever.

'Then came forward the ambassador of the king, and the Adon [of his house, by name . . . . , and presented the ambassadors] of the great king of Kheta, Kheta-sira, who were sent to Pharaoh to propose friendship with the king Ramessu Miamun, the dispenser of life eternally and for ever, just as his father the Sun-god [dispenses it] each day.

'This is the copy of the contents of the silver tablet, which the great king of Kheta, Kheta-sira, had caused to be made, and which was presented to the Pharaoh by the hand of his ambassador Tartisebu and his ambassador Ra-mes, to propose friendship with the king Ramessu Miamun, the bull among the princes, who places his boundary-marks where it pleases him in all lands.

'The treaty which had been proposed by the great king of Kheta, Kheta-sira, the powerful, the son of Maur-sira, the powerful, the son of the son of Sapalil, the great king of Kheta, the powerful, on the silver tablet, to Ramessu Miamun, the great prince of Egypt, the powerful, the son of Meneptah Seti, the great prince of Egypt, the powerful, the son's son of Ramessu I., the great king of Egypt, the powerful,—this was a good treaty for friendship and concord, which assured peace [and established concord] for a longer period than was previously the case, since a long time. For it was the agreement of the great prince of Egypt in common with the great king of Kheta, that the god should not allow enmity to exist between them, on the basis of a treaty.

'To wit, in the times of Mautal, the great king of Kheta, my brother, he was at war with [Meneptah Seti] the great prince of Egypt.

'But now, from this very day forward, Kheta-sira, the great king of Kheta, shall look upon this treaty, so that the agreement may remain, which the god Ra has made, which the god Sutekh has made, for the people of Egypt and for the people of Kheta, that there should be no more enmity between them for evermore.'

And these are the contents :—

'Kheta-sira, the great king of Kheta, is in covenant with Ramessu Miamun, the great prince of Egypt, from this very day forward, that there may subsist a good friendship and a good understanding between them for evermore.

'He shall be my ally ; he shall be my friend : I will be his ally ; I will be his friend : for ever.

'To wit, in the time of Mautal, the great king of Kheta, his brother, after his murder Kheta-sira placed himself on the throne of his father as the great king of Kheta. I strove for friendship with Ramessu Miamun, the great prince of Egypt, and it is [my wish] that the friendship and the concord may be better than the friendship and the concord which before existed, and which was broken.

'I declare: I, the great king of Kheta, will hold together with [Ramessu Miamun], the great prince of Egypt, in good friendship and in good concord. The sons of the sons of the great king of Kheta will hold together and be friends with the sons of the sons of Ramessu Miamun, the great prince of Egypt.

'In virtue of our treaty for concord, and in virtue of our agreement [for friendship, let the people] of Egypt [be united in friendship] with the people of Kheta. Let a like friendship and a like concord subsist in such manner for ever.

'Never let enmity rise between them. Never let the great king of Kheta invade the land of Egypt, if anything shall have been plundered from it. Never let Ramessu Miamun, the great prince of Egypt, over-step the boundary of the land [of Kheta, if anything shall have been plundered] from it.

'The just treaty, which existed in the times of Sapalil, the great king of Kheta, likewise the just treaty which existed in the times of Mautal, the great king of Kheta, my brother, that will I keep.

'Ramessu Miamun, the great prince of Egypt, declares that he will keep it. [We have come to an understanding about it] with one another at the same time from this day forward, and we will fulfil it, and will act in a righteous manner.

'If another shall come as an enemy to the lands of Ramessu Miamun, the great prince of Egypt, then let him send an embassy to the great king of Kheta to this effect: "Come! and make me stronger than him." Then shall the great king of Kheta [assemble his warriors], and the king of Kheta [shall come] to smite his enemies. But if it should not be the wish of the great king of Kheta to march out in person, then he shall send his warriors and his chariots, that they may smite his enemies. Otherwise [he would incur] the wrath of Ramessu Miamun, [the great prince of Egypt. And if Ramessu Miamun, the great prince of Egypt, should banish] for a crime subjects from his country, and they should commit another crime against him, then shall he (the king of Kheta) come forward to kill them. The great king of Kheta shall act in common with [the great prince of Egypt.

'If another should come as an enemy to the lands of the great king of Kheta, then shall he send an embassy to the great prince of Egypt with the request that] he would come in great power to kill his enemies; and if it be the intention of Ramessu Miamun, the great prince of Egypt, to come (himself), he shall [smite the enemies of the great king of Kheta. If it is not the intention of the great prince of Egypt to march out in person, then he shall send his warriors and his two-] horse chariots, while he sends back the answer to the people of Kheta.

'If any subjects of the great king of Kheta have offended him, then Ramessu Miamun, [the great prince of Egypt, shall not receive them in his land, but shall advance to kill them] . . . . the oath, with the wish to say: I will go . . . . until . . . . Ramessu Miamun, the great prince of Egypt, living for ever . . . . that he may be given for them (?) to the lord, and that Ramessu Miamun, the great prince of Egypt, may speak according to his agreement evermore. . . .

'[If servants shall flee away] out of the territories of Ramessu Miamun, the great prince of Egypt, to betake themselves to the great king of Kheta, the great king of Kheta shall not receive them, but the great king of Kheta

C

shall give them up to Ramessu Miamun, the great prince of Egypt, [that they may receive their punishment.

'If servants of Ramessu Miamun, the great prince of Egypt, leave his country], and betake themselves to the land of Kheta, to make themselves servants of another, they shall not remain in the land of Kheta ; [they shall be given up] to Ramessu Miamun, the great prince of Egypt.

'If, on the other hand, there should flee away [servants of the great king of Kheta, in order to betake themselves to] Ramessu Miamun, the great prince of Egypt, [in order to stay in Egypt], then those who have come from the land of Kheta in order to betake themselves to Ramessu Miamun, the great prince of Egypt, shall not be [received by] Ramessu Miamun, the great prince of Egypt, [but] the great prince of Egypt, Ramessu Miamun, [shall deliver them up to the great king of Kheta].

'[And if there shall leave the land of Kheta persons] of skilful mind, so that they come to the land of Egypt to make themselves servants of another, then Ramessu Miamun will not allow them to settle, he will deliver them up to the great king of Kheta.

'When this [treaty] shall be known [by the inhabitants of the land of Egypt and of the land of Kheta, then shall they not offend against it, for all that stands written on] the silver tablet, these are words which will have been approved by the company of the gods among the male gods and among the female gods, among those namely of the land of Egypt. They are witnesses for me [to the validity] of these words, [which they have allowed.

'This is the catalogue of the gods of the land of Kheta :—

(1) 'Sutekh of the city] of Tunep [1],
(2) 'Sutekh of the land of Kheta,
(3) 'Sutekh of the city of Arnema,
(4) 'Sutekh of the city of Zaranda,
(5) 'Sutekh of the city of Pilqa,
(6) 'Sutekh of the city of Khisasap,
(7) 'Sutekh of the city of Sarsu,
(8) 'Sutekh of the city of Khilip (Aleppo),
(9) 'Sutekh of the city of   ,
(10) 'Sutekh of the city of Sarpina,
(11) ' Astarta [2] of the land of Kheta,
(12) 'The god of the land of Zaiath-khirri,
(13) 'The god of the land of Ka . . .,
(14) 'The god of the land of Kher . . .,
(15) 'The goddess of the city of Akh . . .,
(16) '[The goddess of the city of . . .] and of the land
        of A . . ua,
(17) 'The goddess of the land of Zaina,
(18) 'The god of the land of . . nath . . er.

'[I have invoked these male and these] female [gods
of the land of Kheta, these are the gods] of the land,
[as witnesses to] my oath. [With them have been associated the male and the female gods] of the mountains
and of the rivers of the land of Kheta, the gods of the
land of Qazauadana, Amon, Ra, Sutekh, and the male
and female gods of the land of Egypt, of the earth, of
the sea, of the winds, and of the storms.   .

'With regard to the commandment which the silver
tablet contains for the people of Kheta and for the
people of Egypt, he who shall not observe it shall be
given over [to the vengeance] of the company of the

[1] Now Tennib in Northern Syria.
[2] Also read Antarata.

gods of Kheta, and shall be given over [to the ven-
geance] of the gods of Egypt, [he] and his house and
his servants.

'But he who shall observe these commandments
which the silver tablet contains, whether he be of the
people of Kheta or [of the people of Egypt], because
he has not neglected them, the company of the gods
of the land of Kheta and the company of the gods of
the land of Egypt shall secure his reward and preserve
life [for him] and his servants and those who are with
him and who are with his servants.

'If there flee away of the inhabitants [one from the
land of Egypt], or two or three, and they betake themselves to the great king of Kheta [the great king of
Kheta shall not] allow them [to remain, but he shall]
deliver them up, and send them back to Ramessu
Miamun, the great prince of Egypt.

'Now with respect to the [inhabitant of the land of
Egypt], who is delivered up to Ramessu Miamun, the
great prince of Egypt, his fault shall not be avenged
upon him, his [house] shall not be taken away, nor his
[wife] nor his [children]. There shall not be [put to
death his mother, neither shall he be punished in his
eyes, nor on his mouth, nor on the soles of his feet],
so that thus no crime shall be brought forward against
him.

'In the same way shall it be done if inhabitants of
the land of Kheta take to flight, be it one alone, or two,
or three, to betake themselves to Ramessu Miamun, the
great prince of Egypt. Ramessu Miamun, the great
prince of Egypt, shall cause them to be seized, and
they shall be delivered up to the great king of Kheta.

'[With regard to] him who [is delivered up, his crime

shall not be brought forward against him]. His [house] shall not be taken away, nor his wives, nor his children, nor his people; his mother shall not be put to death; he shall not be punished in his eyes, nor on his mouth, nor on the soles of his feet, nor shall any accusation be brought forward against him.

'That which is in the middle of this silver tablet and on its front side is a likeness of the god Sutekh . . . . surrounded by an inscription to this effect: "This is the [picture] of the god Sutekh, the king of heaven and [earth]." At the time (?) of the treaty which Kheta-sira, the great king of the Kheta, made . . . .'

This compact of offensive and defensive alliance proves more forcibly than any description the position to which the Hittite empire had attained. It ranked side by side with the Egypt of Ramses, the last great Pharaoh who ever ruled over the land of the Nile. With Egypt it had contested the sovereignty of Western Asia, and had compelled the Egyptian monarch to consent to peace. Egypt and the Hittites were now the two leading powers of the world.

The treaty was ratified by the visit of the Hittite prince Kheta-sira to Egypt in his national costume, and the marriage of his daughter to Ramses in the thirty-fourth year of the Pharaoh's reign (B. C. 1354). She took the Egyptian name of Ur-maa Noferu-Ra, and her beauty was celebrated by the scribes of the court. Syria was handed over to the Hittites as their legitimate possession; Egypt never again attempted to wrest it from them, and if the Hittite yoke was to be shaken off it must be through the efforts of the Syrians themselves. For a while, however, 'the great king of the Hittites' preserved his power intact; his supremacy was acknowledged from the Euphrates in the east to the Ægean Sea in the west, from Kappadokia in the north to the tribes of Canaan in the south. Even Naharina, once the antagonist of the Egyptian Pharaohs, acknowledged his sovereignty, and Pethor, the home of Balaam, at the junction of the Euphrates and the Sajur, became a Hittite town. The cities of Philistia, indeed, still sent tribute to the Egyptian ruler, but northwards the Hittite sway seems to have been omnipotent. The Amorites of the mountains allied themselves with 'the children of Heth,' and the Canaanites in the lowlands looked to them for protection. The Israelites had not as yet thrust themselves between the two great powers of the Oriental world : it was still possible for a Hittite sovereign to visit Egypt, and for an Egyptian traveller to explore the cities of Canaan.

After sixty-six years of vainglorious splendour the long reign of Ramses II. came to an end (B. C. 1322). The Israelites had toiled for him in building Pithom and Raamses, and on the accession of his son and successor, Meneptah, they demanded permission to depart from Egypt. The history of the Exodus is too well known to be recounted here ; it marks the close of the period of conquest and prosperity which Egypt had enjoyed under the kings of the eighteenth and nineteenth dynasties. Early in his reign Meneptah had sent corn by sea to the Hittites at a time when there was a famine in Syria, showing that the peaceful relations established during the reign of his father were still in force. Despatches dated in his third year also exist, which speak of letters and messengers passing to and fro between Egypt and Phœnicia, and make it clear that Gaza was still garrisoned by Egyptian troops. But in the fifth year of his reign Egypt was invaded by a confederacy of white-skinned tribes from Libya and the shores of Asia Minor, who overran the Delta and threatened the very existence of the Egyptian monarchy. Egypt, however, was saved by a battle in which the invading host was almost annihilated, but not before it had itself been half drained of its resources, and weakened correspondingly.

Not many years afterwards the dynasty of Ramses the Oppressor descended to its grave in bloodshed and disaster. Civil war broke out, followed by foreign invasion, and the crown was seized by 'Arisu the Phœnician.' But happier times again arrived. Once more the Egyptians obeyed a native prince, and the Twentieth Dynasty was founded. Its one great king was Ramses III., who rescued his country from two invasions more formidable even than that which had been beaten back by Meneptah. Like the latter, they were conducted by the Libyans and the nations of the Greek seas, and the invaders were defeated partly on the land, partly on the water. The maritime confederacy included the Teukrians of the Troad, the Lykians and the Philistines, perhaps also the natives of Sardinia and Sicily. They had flung themselves in the first instance on the coasts of Phœnicia, and spread inland as far as Carchemish. Laden with spoil, they fixed their camp 'in the land of the Amorites,' and then descended upon Egypt. The Hittites of Carchemish and the people of Matenau of Naharina came in their train, and a long and terrible battle took place on the sea-shore between Raphia and Pelusium. The Egyptians were victorious ; the ships of the enemy were sunk, and their soldiers slain or captured. Egypt was once more filled with captives, and the flame of its former glory flickered again for a moment before finally going out.

The list of prisoners shows that the Hittite tribes had taken part in the struggle, Carchemish, Aleppo, and Pethor being specially named as having sent contingents to the war. They had probably marched by land, while their allies from Asia Minor and the islands of the Mediterranean had attacked the Egyptian coast in ships. So far as we can gather, the Hittite populations no longer acknowledged the suzerainty of an imperial sovereign, but were divided into independent states. It would seem, too, that they had lost their hold upon Mysia and the far west. The Tsekkri and the Leku, the Shardaina and the Shakalsha are said to have attacked their cities before proceeding on their southward march. If we can trust the statement, we must conclude that the Hittite empire had already broken up. The tribes of Asia Minor it had conquered were in revolt, and had carried the war into the homes of their former masters. However this may be, it is certain that from this time forward the power of the Hittites in Syria began to wane. Little by little the Aramæan population pushed them back into their northern fastnesses, and throughout the period of the Israelitish judges we never hear even of their name. The Hittite chieftains advance no longer to the south of Kadesh ; and though Israel was once oppressed by a king who had come from the north, he was king of Aram-Naharaim, the Naharina of the Egyptian texts, and not a Hittite prince.

Where the Egyptian monuments desert us, those of Assyria come to our help. The earliest notices of the Hittites found in the cuneiform texts are contained in a great work on astronomy and astrology, originally compiled for an early king of Babylonia. The references to 'the king of the Hittites,' however, which meet us in it, cannot be ascribed to a remote date. One of the chief objects aimed at by the author (or authors) of the work was to foretell the future, it being supposed that a particular event which had followed a certain celestial phenomenon would be repeated when the phenomenon happened again. Consequently it was the fashion to introduce into the work from time to time fresh notices of events ; and some of these glosses, as we may term them, are probably not older than the seventh century B. C. It is, therefore, impossible to determine the exact date to which the allusions to the Hittite king belong, but there are indications that it is comparatively late. The first clear account that the Assyrian inscriptions give us concerning the Hittites, to which we can attach a date, is met with in the annals of Tiglath-pileser I.

Tiglath-pileser I. was the most famous monarch of the first Assyrian empire, and he reigned about 1110 B. C. He carried his arms northward and westward, pene-trating into the bleak and trackless mountains of Armenia, and forcing his way as far as Malatiyeh in Kappadokia. His annals present us with a very full and interesting picture of the geography of these regions at the time of his reign. Kummukh or Komagene, which at that epoch extended southward from Malatiyeh in the direction of Carchemish, was one of the first objects of his attack. 'At the beginning of my reign,' he says, ' 20,000 Moschians (or men of Meshech) and their five kings, who for fifty years had taken possession of the countries of Alzi and Purukuzzi, which had formerly paid tribute and taxes to Assur my lord—no king (before me) had opposed them in battle—trusted to their strength, and came down and seized the land of Kummukh.' The Assyrian king, however, marched against them, and defeated them in a pitched battle with great slaughter, and then proceeded to carry fire and sword through the cities of Kummukh. Its ruler Kili-anteru, the son of Kali-anteru, was captured along with his wives and family ; and Tiglath-pileser next proceeded to besiege the stronghold of Urrakhinas. Its prince Sadi-anteru, the son of Khattukhi, 'the Hittite,' threw himself at the conqueror's feet ; his life was spared, and 'the wide-spreading land of Kummukh' became tributary to Assyria, objects of bronze being the chief articles it had to offer. About the same time, 4000 troops belonging to the Kaska or Kolkhians and the people of Uruma, both of whom are described as 'soldiers of the Hittites' and as having occupied the northern cities of Mesopotamia, submitted voluntarily to the Assyrian monarch, and were transported to Assyria along with their chariots and their property. Uruma was the Urima of classical geography, which lay on the Euphrates a little to the north of Birejik, so that we know the exact locality to which these 'Hittite soldiers' belonged. In fact, 'Hittite' must have been a general name given to the inhabitants of all this district; the modern Merash, for instance, lies within the limits of the ancient Kummukh ; and, as we shall see, it is from Merash that a long Hittite inscription has come.

Tiglath-pileser attacked Kummukh a second time, and on this occasion penetrated still further into the mountain fastnesses of the Hittite country. In a third campaign his armies came in sight of Malatiyeh itself, but the king contented himself with exacting a small yearly tribute from the city, 'having had pity upon it, as he tells us, though more probably the truth was that he found himself unable to take it by storm. But he never succeeded in forcing his way across the fords of the Euphrates, which were commanded by the great fortress of Carchemish. Once he harried the land of Mitanni or Naharina, slaying and spoiling ' in one day' from Carchemish southwards to a point that faced the deserts of the nomad ·Sukhi, the Shuhites of the Book of Job. It was on this occasion that he killed ten elephants in the neighbourhood of Harran and on the banks of the Khabour, besides four wild bulls which he hunted with arrows and spears ' in the land of Mitanni and in the city of Araziqi[1], which lies opposite to the land of the Hittites.'

Towards the end of the twelfth century before our era, therefore, the Hittites were still strong enough to keep one of the mightiest of the Assyrian kings in check. It is true that they no longer obeyed a single head ; it is also true that that portion of them which was settled in the land of Kummukh was overrun by the Assyrian armies, and forced to pay tribute to the Assyrian invader. But Carchemish compelled the respect of Tiglath-pileser; he never ventured to approach its walls or to cross the river which it was intended to defend. His way was barred to the west, and he never succeeded in traversing the high road which led to Phœnicia and Palestine.

After the death of Tiglath-pileser I. the Assyrian inscriptions fail us. His successors allowed the empire to fall into decay, and more than two hundred years elapsed before the curtain is lifted again. These two hundred years had witnessed the rise and fall of the

---

[1] Called Eragiza in classical geography and in the Talmud.

kingdom of David and Solomon as well as the growth of a new power, that of the Syrians of Damascus.

Damascus rose on the ruins of the empire of Solomon. But its rise also shows plainly that the power of the Hittites in Syria was beginning to wane. Hadad-ezer, king of Zobah, the antagonist of David, had been able to send for aid to the Arameans of Naharina, on the eastern side of the Euphrates (2 Sam. x. 16), and with them he had marched to Helam, in which it is possible to see the name of Aleppo[1]. It is clear that the Hittites were no longer able to keep the Aramean population in subjection, or to prevent an Aramean prince of Zobah from expelling them from the territory they had once made their own. Indeed, it may be that in one passage of the Old Testament allusion is made to an attack which Hadad-ezer was preparing against them. When it is stated that he was overthrown by David, 'as he was going to turn his hand against the river Euphrates' (2 Sam. viii. 3), it may be that it was against the Hittites of Carchemish that his armies were about to be directed. At any rate, support for this view is found in a further statement of the sacred historian. 'When Toi king of Hamath,' we learn, 'heard that David had smitten all the host of Hadad-ezer, then Toi sent Joram his son unto king David, to salute him, and to bless him, because he had fought against Hadad-ezer and smitten him; for Hadad-ezer had wars with Toi' (2 Sam. viii. 9, 10). Now we know from the monuments that have been discovered on the spot that Hamath was once a Hittite city, and there is no reason for not believing that it was still in the possession of the Hittites in the

[1] Called Khalman in the Assyrian texts. Josephus changes Helam into the proper name Khalaman.

age of David. Its Syrian enemies would in that case have been the same as the enemies of David, and a common danger would thus have united it with Israel in an alliance which ended only in its overthrow by the Assyrians.

As late as the time of Uzziah, we are told by the Assyrian inscriptions, the Jewish king was in league with Hamath, and the 'last independent ruler of Hamath was Yahu-bihdi, a name in which we recognise that of the God of Israel. Indeed, the very fact that the Syrians imagined that 'the kings of the Hittites' were coming to the rescue of Samaria, when besieged by the forces of Damascus, goes to show that Israel and the Hittites were regarded as natural friends, whose natural adversaries were the Arameans of Syria. As the power and growth of Israel had been built up on the conquest and subjugation of the Semitic populations of Palestine, so too the power of the Hittites had been gained at the expense of their Semitic neighbours. The triumph of Syria was a blow alike to the Hittites of Carchemish and to the Hebrews of Samaria and Jerusalem.

With Assur-natsir-pal, whose reign extended from B.C. 885 to 860, contemporaneous Assyrian history begins afresh. His campaigns and conquests rivalled those of Tiglath-pileser I., and indeed exceeded them both in extent and in brutality. Like his predecessor, he exacted tribute from Kummukh as well as from the kings of the country in which Malatiyeh was situated ; but with better fortune than Tiglath-pileser he succeeded in passing the Euphrates, and obliging Sangara of Carchemish to pay him homage. It is clear that Carchemish was no longer as strong as it had been two centuries before, and that the power of its defenders was gradually

vanishing away.   There was still, however, a small
Hittite population on the eastern bank of the Euphrates;
at all events, Assur-natsir-pal describes the tribe of
Bakhian on that side of the river as Hittite, and it was
only after receiving tribute from them that he crossed
the stream in boats and approached the land of Gargamis or Carchemish.   But his threatened assault upon
the Hittite stronghold was bought off with rich and
numerous presents.   Twenty talents of silver — the
favourite metal of the Hittite princes—'cups of gold,
chains of gold, blades of gold, 100 talents of copper,
250 talents of iron, gods of copper in the form of wild
bulls, bowls of copper, libation cups of copper, a ring of
copper, the multitudinous furniture of the royal palace,
of which the like was never received, couches and
thrones of rare woods and ivory, 200 slave-girls, gar-
ments of variegated cloth and linen, masses of black
crystal and blue crystal, precious stones, the tusks of
elephants, a white chariot, small images of gold,' as well
as ordinary chariots and war-horses, — such were the
treasures poured into the lap of the Assyrian monarch
by the wealthy but unwarlike king of Carchemish.   They
give us an idea of the wealth to which the city had
attained through its favourable position on the high-
road of commerce that ran from the east to the west.
The uninterrupted prosperity of several centuries had
filled it with merchants and riches ; in later days we
find the Assyrian inscriptions speaking of 'the maneh
of Carchemish' as one of the recognised standards of
value.   Carchemish had become a city of merchants,
and no longer felt itself able to oppose by arms the
trained warriors of the Assyrian king.   .
    Quitting Carchemish, Assur-natsir-pal pursued his

march westwards, and after passing the land of Akhanu on his left, fell upon the town of Azaz near Aleppo, which belonged to the king of the Patinians. The latter people were of Hittite descent, and occupied the country between the river Afrin and the shores of the Gulf of Antioch. The Assyrian armies crossed the Afrin and appeared before the walls of the Patinian capital. Large bribes, however, induced them to turn away southward, and to advance along the Orontes in the direction of the Lebanon. Here Assur-natsir-pal received the tribute of the Phœnician cities.

Shalmaneser II., the son and successor of Assur-natsir-pal, continued the warlike policy of his father (B.C. 860–825). The Hittite princes were again a special object of attack. Year after year Shalmaneser led his armies against them, and year after year did he return home laden with spoil. The aim of his policy is not difficult to discover. He sought to break the power of the Hittite race in Syria, to possess himself of the fords across the Euphrates and the high-road which brought the merchandise of Phœnicia to the traders of Nineveh, and eventually to divert the commerce of the Mediterranean to his own country. By the overthrow of the Patinians he made himself master of the cedar forests of Amanus, and his palaces were erected with the help of their wood. Sangara of Carchemish, it is true, perceived his danger, and a league of the Hittite princes was formed to resist the common foe. Contingents came not only from Kummukh and from the Patinians, but from Cilicia and the mountain ranges of Asia Minor. It was, however, of no avail. The Hittite forces were driven from the field, and their leaders were compelled to purchase peace by the payment of tribute. Once more Carchemish gave up its gold and silver, its bronze and copper, its purple vestures and curiously-adorned thrones, and the daughter of Sangara himself was carried away to the harem of the Assyrian king. Pethor, the city of Balaam, was turned into an Assyrian colony, its very name being changed to an Assyrian one. The way into Hamath and Phœnicia at last lay open to the Assyrian host. At Aleppo Shalmaneser offered sacrifices to the native god Hadad, and then descended upon the cities of Hamath. At Karkar he was met by a great confederacy formed by the kings of Hamath and Damascus, to which Ahab of Israel had contributed 2000 chariots and 10,000 men. But nothing could withstand the onslaught of the Assyrian veterans. The enemy were scattered like chaff, and the river Orontes was reddened with their blood. The battle of Karkar (in B.C. 854) brought the Assyrians into contact with Damascus, and caused Jehu on a later occasion to send tribute to the Assyrian king.

The subsequent history of Shalmaneser concerns us but little. The power of the Hittites south of the Taurus had been broken for ever. The Semite had avenged himself for the conquest of his country by the northern mountaineers centuries before. They no longer formed a barrier which cut off the east from the west, and prevented the Semites of Assyria and Babylon from meeting the Semites of Phœnicia and Palestine. The intercourse which had been interrupted in the age of the nineteenth dynasty of Egypt could now be again resumed. Carchemish ceased to command the fords of the Euphrates, and was forced to acknowledge the supremacy of the Assyrian invader. In fact, the Hittites of Syria had become little more than tributaries of the

Assyrian monarch. When an insurrection broke out among the Patinians, in consequence of which the rightful king was killed and his throne seized by an usurper, Shalmaneser claimed and exercised the right to interfere. A new sovereign was appointed by him, and he set up an image of himself in the capital city of the Patinian people.

The change that had come over the relations between the Assyrians and the Hittite population is marked by a curious fact. From the time of Shalmaneser onwards, the name of Hittite is no longer used by the Assyrian writers in a correct sense. It is extended so as to embrace all the inhabitants of Northern Syria on the western side of the Euphrates, and subsequently came to include the inhabitants of Palestine as well. Khatta or 'Hittite' became synonymous with Syrian. How this happened is not difficult to explain. The first populations of Syria with whom the Assyrians had come into contact were of Hittite origin. When their power was broken, and the Assyrian armies had forced their way past the barrier they had so long presented to the invader, it was natural that the states next traversed by the Assyrian generals should be supposed also to belong to them. Moreover, many of these states were actually dependent on the Hittite princes, though inhabited by an Aramean people. The Hittites had imposed their yoke upon an alien race of Aramean descent, and accordingly in Northern Syria Hittite and Aramean cities and tribes were intermingled together. 'I took,' says Shalmaneser, 'what the men of the land of the Hittites had called the city of Pethor (*Pitru*), which is upon the river Sajur (*Sagura*), on the further side of the Euphrates, and the city of Mudkînu, on the eastern side of the Euphrates, which Tiglath-pileser (I.), the royal forefather who went before me, had united to my country, and Assur-rab-buri king of Assyria and the king of the Arameans had taken (from it) by a treaty.' At a later date Shalmaneser marched from Pethor to Aleppo, and there offered sacrifices to 'the god of the city,' Hadad-Rimmon, whose name betrays the Semitic character of its population. The Hittites, in short, had never been more than a conquering upper class in Syria, like the Normans in Sicily; and as time went on the subject population gained more and more upon them. Like all similar aristocracies, they tended to die out or to be absorbed into the native population of the country.

They still held possession of Carchemish, however, and the decadence of the first Assyrian empire gave them an unexpected respite. But the revolution which placed Tiglath-pileser III. on the throne of Assyria, in B.C. 725, brought with it the final doom of Hittite supremacy. Assyria entered upon a new career of conquest, and under its new rulers established an empire which extended over the whole of Western Asia. In B.C. 717 Carchemish finally fell before the armies of Sargon, and its last king Pisiris became the captive of the Assyrian king. Its trade and wealth passed into Assyrian hands, it was colonised by Assyrians and placed under an Assyrian satrap. The great Hittite stronghold on the Euphrates, which had been for so many centuries the visible sign of their power and southern conquests, became once more the possession of a Semitic people. The long struggle that had been carried on between the Hittites and the Semites was at an end ; the Semite had triumphed, and the Hittite was driven back into the mountains from whence he had come.

But he did not yield without a struggle. The year following the capture of Carchemish saw Sargon confronted by a great league of the northern peoples, Meshech, Tubal, Melitene and others, under the leadership of the king of Ararat. The league, however, was shattered in a decisive battle, the king of Ararat committed suicide, and in less than three years Komagene was annexed to the Assyrian empire. The Semite of Nineveh was supreme in the Eastern world.

Ararat was the name given by the Assyrians to the district in the immediate neighbourhood of Lake Van, as well as to the country to the south of it. It was not until post-Biblical days that the name was extended to the north, so that the modern Mount Ararat obtained a title which originally belonged to the Kurdish range in the south. But Ararat was not the native name of the country. This was Biainas or Bianas, a name which still survives in that of Lake Van. Numerous inscriptions are scattered over the country, written in cuneiform characters borrowed from Nineveh in the time of Assur-natsir-pal or his son Shalmaneser, but in a language which bears no resemblance to that of Assyria. They record the building of temples and palaces, the offerings made to the gods, and the campaigns of the Vannic kings. Among the latter mention is made of campaigns against the Khate or Hittites.

The first of these campaigns was conducted by a king called Menuas, who reigned in the ninth century before our era. He overran the land of Alzi, and then found himself in the land of the Hittites. Here he plundered the cities of Surisilis and Tarkhi-gamas,

belonging to the Hittite prince Sada-halis, and captured
a number of soldiers, whom he dedicated to the service
of his god Khaldis.   On another occasion he marched
as far as the city of Malatiyeh, and after passing through
the country of the Hittites, caused an inscription com-
memorating his conquests to be engraved on the cliffs
of Palu.   Palu is situated on the northern bank of the
Euphrates, about midway between Malatiyeh and Van,
and as it lies to the east of the ancient district of Alzi,
we can form some idea of the exact geographical
position to which the Hittites of Menuas must be
assigned.   His son and successor, Argistis I, again made
war upon them, and we gather from one of his inscriptions that the city of Malatiyeh was itself included
among their fortresses.   The 'land of the Hittites,'
according to the statements of the Vannic kings, stretched
along the banks of the Euphrates from Palu on the
east as far as Malatiyeh on the west.

The Hittites of the Assyrian monuments lived to the
south-west of this region, spreading through Komagene
to Carchemish and Aleppo.   The Egyptian records
bring them yet further south to Kadesh on the Orontes,
while the Old Testament carries the name into the
extreme south of Palestine.   It is evident, therefore,
that we must see in the Hittite tribes fragments of a
race whose original seat was in the ranges of the Taurus,
but who had pushed their way into the warm plains
and valleys of Syria and Palestine.   They belonged
originally to Asia Minor, not to Syria, and it was
conquest only which gave them a right to the name
of Syrians.   'Hittite' was their true title, and whether
the tribes to which it belonged lived in Judah or on
the Orontes, at Carchemish or in the neighbourhood of

Palu, this was the title under which they were known. We must regard it as a national name, which clung to them in all their conquests and migrations, and marked them out as a peculiar people, distinct from the other races of the Eastern world. It is now time to see what their own monuments have to tell us regarding them, and the influence they exercised upon the history of mankind.

A SLAB FOUND AT MERASH.

CHAPTER III.

THE HITTITE MONUMENTS.

IT was a warm and sunny September morning when
I left the little town of Nymphi near Smyrna with
a strong escort of Turkish soldiers, and made my way
to the Pass of Karabel. The Pass of Karabel is a
narrow defile, shut in on either side by lofty cliffs,
through which ran the ancient road from Ephesos in
the south to Sardes and Smyrna in the north. The
Greek historian Herodotos tells us that the Egyptian
conqueror Sesostris had left memorials of himself in
this place. 'Two images cut by him in the rock' were
to be seen beside the roads which led 'from Ephesos

to Phokaea and from Sardes to Smyrna. On either side a man is carved, a little over three feet in height, who holds a spear in the right hand and a bow in the left. The rest of his accoutrement is similar, for it is Egyptian and Ethiopian, and from one shoulder to the other, right across the breast, Egyptian hieroglyphics have been cut which declare : " I have won this land with my shoulders."'

These two images were the object of my journey. One of them had been discovered by Renouard in 1839, and shortly afterwards sketched by Texier ; the other had been found by Dr. Beddoe in 1856. But visitors to the Pass in which they were engraved were few and far between ; the cliffs on either side were the favourite haunt of brigands, and thirty soldiers were not deemed too many to protect my safety. My work of exploration had to be carried on under the shelter of their guns, for more than twenty bandits were lurking under the brushwood above.

The sculpture sketched by Texier had subsequently been photographed by Mr. Svoboda. It represents a warrior whose height is rather more than life-size, and who stands in profile with the right foot planted in front of nim, in the attitude of one who is marching. In his right hand he holds a spear, behind his left shoulder is slung a bow, and the head is crowned with a high peaked cap. He is clad in a tunic which reaches to the knees, and his feet are shod with boots with turned-up ends. The whole figure is cut in deep relief in an artificial niche, and between the spear and the face are three lines of hieroglyphic characters. The figure faces south, and is carved on the face of the eastern cliff of Karabel.

It had long been recognised that the hieroglyphics were not those of Egypt, and Professor Perrot had also drawn attention to the striking resemblance between the style of art represented by this sculpture and that represented by certain rock-sculptures in Kappadokia, as well as by the sculptured image of a warrior discovered by himself at a place called Ghiaur-kalessi, ' the castle of the infidel,' in Phrygia, which is practically identical in form and character with the sculptured warrior of Karabel.

What was the origin of this art, or who were the people it commemorated, was a matter of uncertainty. A few weeks, however, before my visit to the Pass of Karabel, I announced[1] that I had come to the conclusion that the art was Hittite, and that the hieroglyphics accompanying the figure at Karabel would turn out, when carefully examined, to be Hittite also. The primary purpose of my visit to the pass was to verify this conclusion.

Let us now see how I had arrived at it. The story is a long one, and in order to understand it, it is necessary to transport ourselves from the Pass of Karabel in Western Asia Minor to Hamah, the site of the ancient Hamath, in the far east. It was here that the first discovery was made which has led by slow degrees to the reconstruction of the Hittite empire, and a recognition of the important part once played by the Hittites in the history of the civilised world.

As far back as the beginning of the present century (in 1812) the great Oriental traveller Burckhardt had noticed a block of black basalt covered with strange-looking hieroglyphics built into the corner of a house

[1] In the *Academy* of Aug. 16th, 1879.

in one of the bazaars of Hamah[1]. But the discovery was forgotten, and the European residents in Hamah, like the travellers who visited the city, were convinced that 'no antiquities' were to be found there. Nearly sixty years later, however, when the American Palestine Exploration Society was first beginning its work, the American consul, Mr. Johnson, and an American missionary, Mr. Jessup, accidentally lighted again upon this stone, and further learned that three other stones of similar character, and inscribed with similar hieroglyphics, existed elsewhere in Hamah. One of them, of very great length, was believed to be endowed with healing properties. Rheumatic patients, Mohammedans and Christians alike, were in the habit of stretching themselves upon it, in the firm belief that their pains would be absorbed into the stone. The other inscribed stones were also regarded with veneration, which naturally increased when it was known that they were being sought after by the Franks ; and the two Americans found it impossible to see them all, much less to take copies of the inscriptions they bore. They had to be content with the miserable attempts at reproducing them made by a native painter, one of which was afterwards published in America. The publication served to awaken the interest of scholars in the newly discovered inscriptions, and efforts were made by Sir Richard Burton and others to obtain correct impressions of them. All was in vain, however, and it is probable that the fanaticism or greed of the people of Hamah would have successfully resisted all attempts to procure trustworthy copies of the texts, had not a lucky accident brought Dr. William Wright to the spot. It is to his

[1] *Travels in Syria*, p. 146.

energy and devotion that the preservation of these
precious relics of Hittite literature may be said to be
due. 'On the 10th of November, 1872,' he tells us,
he 'set out from Damascus, intent on securing the
Hamah inscriptions. The Sublime Porte, seized by
a periodic fit of reforming zeal, had appointed an honest
man, Subhi Pasha, to be governor of Syria. Subhi Pasha
brought a conscience to his work, and, not content with
redressing wrongs that succeeded in forcing their way
into his presence, resolved to visit every district of his
province, in order that he might check the spoiler and
discover the wants of the people. He invited me to
accompany him on a tour to Hamah, and I gladly
accepted the invitation.' Along with Mr. Green, the
English Consul, accordingly, Dr. Wright joined the
party of the Pasha; and, fearing that the same fate might
befall the Hamath stones as had befallen the Moabite
Stone, which had been broken into pieces to save it
from the Europeans, persuaded him to buy them, and
send them as a present to the Museum at Constantinople. When the news became known in Hamah,
there were murmurings long and deep against the
Pasha, and it became necessary, not only to appeal
to the cupidity and fear of the owners of the stones,
but also to place them under the protection of a guard
of soldiers the night before the work of removing them
was to commence.

The night was an anxious one to Dr. Wright ; but
when day dawned, the stones were still safe, and the
labour of their removal was at once begun. It 'was
effected by an army of shouting men, who kept the
city in an uproar during the whole day. Two of them
had to be taken out of the walls of inhabited houses,

and one of them was so large that it took fifty men and four oxen a whole day to drag it a mile. The other stones were split in two, and the inscribed parts were carried on the backs of camels to the' court of the governor's palace. Here they could be cleaned and copied at leisure and in safety.

But the work of cleaning them from the accumulated dirt of ages occupied· the greater part of two days. Then came the task of making casts of the inscriptions, with the help of gypsum which some natives had been bribed to bring from the neighbourhood. At length, however, the work was completed, and Dr. Wright had the satisfaction of sending home to England two sets of casts of these ancient and mysterious texts, one for the British Museum, the other for the Palestine Exploration Fund, while the originals themselves were safely deposited in the Museum of Constantinople. It was now time to inquire what the inscriptions meant, and who could have been the authors of them.

Dr. Wright at once suggested that they were the work of the Hittites, and that they were memorials of Hittite writing. But his suggestion was buried in the pages of a periodical better known to theologians than to Orientalists; and the world agreed to call the writing by the name of Hamathite. It specially attracted the notice of Dr. Hayes Ward of New York, who discovered that the inscriptions were written in *boustrophedon* fashion, that is to say, that the lines turned alternately from right to left and from left to right, like oxen when plowing a field, the first line beginning on the right and the line following on the left. The lines read, in fact, from the direction towards which the characters look.

. Dr. Hayes Ward also made another discovery. In

the ruins of the great palace of Nineveh Sir A. H. Layard had discovered numerous clay impressions of seals once attached to documents of papyrus or parchment. The papyrus and parchment have long since perished, but the seals remain, with the holes through which the strings passed that attached them to the original deeds. Some of the seals are Assyrian, some Phœnician, others again are Egyptian, but there are a few which have upon them strange characters such as had never been met with before. It was these characters which Dr. Hayes Ward perceived to be the same as those found upon the stones of Hamah, and it was accordingly supposed that the seals were of Hamathite origin.

In 1876, two years after the publication of Dr. Wright's article, of which I had never heard at the time, I read a Paper on the Hamathite inscriptions before the Society of Biblical Archæology. In this I put forward a number of conjectures, one of them being that the Hamathite hieroglyphs were the source of the curious syllabary used for several centuries in the island of Cyprus, and another that the hieroglyphs were not an invention of the early inhabitants of Hamath, but represented the system of writing employed by the Hittites. We know from the Egyptian records that the Hittites could write, and that a class of scribes existed among them, and, since Hamath lay close to the borders of the Hittite kingdoms, it seemed reasonable to suppose that the unknown form of script discovered on its site was Hittite rather than Hamathite. The conjecture was confirmed almost immediately afterwards by the discovery of the site of Carchemish, the great Hittite capital, and of inscriptions there in the same system of writing as that found on the stones of Hamah.

It was not long, therefore, before the learned world began to recognise that the newly-discovered script was the peculiar possession of the Hittite race. Dr. Hayes Ward was one of the first to do so, and the Trustees of the British Museum determined to institute excavations among the ruins of Carchemish. Meanwhile notice was drawn to a fact which showed that the Hittite characters, as we shall now call them, were employed, not only at Hamath and Carchemish, but in Asia Minor as well.

More than a century ago a German traveller had observed two figures carved on a wall of rock near Ibreez, or Ivris, in the territory of the ancient Lykaonia. One of them was a god, who carried in his hand a stalk of corn and a bunch of grapes, the other was a man, who stood before the god in an attitude of adoration. Both figures were shod with boots with upturned ends, and the deity wore a tunic that reached to his knees, while on his head was a peaked cap ornamented with horn-like ribbons. A century elapsed before the sculpture was again visited by an European traveller, and it was again a German who found his way to the spot. On this occasion a drawing was made of the figures, which was published by Ritter in his great work on the geography of the world. But the drawing was poor and imperfect, and the first attempt to do adequate justice to the original was made by the Rev. E. J. Davis in 1875. He published his copy, and an account of the monument, in the *Transactions of the Society of Biblical Archæology* the following year. He had noticed that the figures were accompanied by what were known at the time as Hamathite characters. Three lines of these were inserted between the face of the god and his uplifted left arm, four lines more were engraved behind his wor-

shipper, while below, on a level with an aqueduct which
fed a mill, were yet other lines of half-obliterated
hieroglyphs. It was plain that in Lykaonia also, where
the old language of the country still lingered in the days
of St. Paul, the Hittite system of writing had once been
used.

Another stone inscribed with Hittite characters had
come to light at Aleppo. Like those of Hamath, it was
of black basalt, and had been built into a modern wall.
The characters upon it were worn by frequent attrition,
the people of Aleppo believing that whoever rubbed his
eyes upon it would be immediately cured of ophthalmia.
More than one copy of the inscription was taken, but
the difficulty of distinguishing the half-obliterated characters rendered the copies of little service, and a cast of
the stone was about to be made when news arrived that
the fanatics of Aleppo had destroyed it. Rather than
allow its virtue to go out of it—to be stolen, as they
fancied, by the Europeans—they preferred to break it in
pieces. It is one of the many monuments that have
perished at the very moment when their importance
first became known.

This, then, was the state of our knowledge in the
summer of 1879. We knew that the Hittites, with
whom Hebrews and Egyptians and Assyrians had once
been in contact, possessed a hieroglyphic system of
writing, and that this system of writing was found on
monuments in Hamath, Aleppo, Carchemish, and Lykaonia. We knew, too, that in Lykaonia it accompanied
figures carved out of the rock in a peculiar style of art,
and represented as wearing a peculiar kind of dress.

Suddenly the truth flashed upon me. This peculiar
style of art, this peculiar kind of dress, was the same as

that which distinguished the sculptures of Karabel, of Ghiaur-kalessi, and of Kappadokia. In all alike we had the same characteristic features, the same head-dresses and shoes, the same tunics, the same clumsy massiveness of design and characteristic attitude. The figures carved upon the rocks of Karabel and Kappadokia must be memorials of Hittite art. The clue to their origin and history was at last discovered ; the birthplace of the strange art which had produced them was made manifest. A little further research made the fact doubly sure. The photographs Professor Perrot had taken of the monuments of Boghaz Keui in Kappadokia included one of an inscription in ten or eleven lines. The characters of this inscription were worn and almost illegible, but not only were they in relief, like the characters of all other Hittite inscriptions known at the time, among them two or three hieroglyphs stood out clearly, which were identical with those on the stones of Hamath and Carchemish. All that was needed to complete the verification of my discovery was to visit the Pass of Karabel, and see whether the hieroglyphs Texier and others had found there likewise belonged to the Hittite script.

More than three hours did I spend in the niche wherein the figure is carved which Herodotos believed was a likeness of the Egyptian Sesostris. It was necessary to take 'squeezes' as well as copies, if I would recover the characters of the inscription and ascertain their exact forms. My joy was great at finding that they were Hittite, and that the conclusion I had arrived at in my study at home was confirmed by the monument itself. The Sesostris of Herodotos turned out to be, not the great Pharaoh who contended with the Hittites of Kadesh, but a symbol of the far-reaching power and

E

influence of his mighty opponents. Hittite art and
Hittite writing, if not the Hittite name, were proved to
have been known from the banks of the Euphrates to
the shores of the Ægean Sea.

The stone warrior of Karabel stands in his niche in
the cliff at a considerable height above the path, and
the direction in which he is marching is that which
would have led him to Ephesos and the Mæander.
His companion lies below, the block of stone out of
which the second figure has been carved having been
apparently shaken by an earthquake from the rocks
above. This second figure is a duplicate of the first.
Both stand in the same position, both are shod with the
same snow-shoes, and both are armed with spear and
bow. But the second figure has suffered much from the
ill-usage of man. The upper part has been purposely
chipped away, and it is not many years ago since a
Yuruk's tent was pitched against the block of stone out
of which it is carved, the niche in which the old warrior
stands conveniently serving as the fire-place of the
family. No trace of inscription remains, if indeed it
ever existed. At any rate, it could not have run across
the breast, as Herodotos asserts.

The account, indeed, given by Herodotos of these two
figures can hardly have been that of an eye-witness.
Instead of being little over three feet in height, they
are more than life-size, and they hold their spears not in
the right but in the left hand. Their accoutrement,
moreover, is as unlike that of an 'Egyptian and Ethiopian'
as it well could be, while the inscription is not traced
across the breast, but between the face and the arm.
Nor was the Greek historian correct in saying that the
pass which the two warriors seem to guard leads not

THE PSEUDO-SESOSTRIS, CARVED ON THE ROCK IN THE PASS OF KARABEL.

only from Ephesos to Phokæa, but also from Sardes
to Smyrna. It is not until the pass is cleared at its
northern end that the road which runs through it—the
Karabel-déré, as the Turks now call it—joins the *Bel-
kaive*, or road from Sardes to Smyrna. It is evident that
Herodotos must have received his account of the figures
from another authority, though his identification of them
with the Egyptian Sesostris is his own.

Not far from Karabel another monument of Hittite
art has been discovered. Hard by the town of Magnesia,
on the lofty cliffs of Sipylos, a strange figure has been
carved out of the rock. It represents a woman with
long locks of hair streaming down her shoulders, and
a jewel like a lotus-flower upon the head, who sits on
a throne in a deep artificial niche. Lydian historians
narrate that it was the image of the daughter of Assaon,
who had sought death by casting herself down from
a precipice ; but Greek legend preferred to see in it the
figure of 'weeping Niobe' turned to stone. Already
Homer told how Niobe, when her twelve children had
been slain by the gods, 'now changed to stone, broods
over the woes the gods had brought, there among the
rocks, in lonely mountains, even in Sipylos, where they
say are the couches of the nymphs who dance on the
banks of the Akheloios.' But it was only after the
settlement of the Greeks in Lydia that the old monument on Mount Sipylos was held to be the image of
Niobe. The limestone rock out of which it was carved
dripped with moisture after rain, and as the water flowed
over the face of the figure, disintegrating and disfiguring
the stone as it ran, the pious Greek beheld in it the
Niobe of his own mythology. The figure was originally
that of the great goddess of Asia Minor, known some-

times as Atergatis or Derketo, sometimes as Kybelê, sometimes by other names. It is difficult for one who has seen the image of Nofert-ari, the favourite wife of Ramses II., seated in the niche of rock on the cliffs of Abu-simbel, not to believe that the artist who carved the image on Mount Sipylos had visited the Nile. At a little distance both have the same appearance, and a nearer examination shows that, although the Egyptian work is finer than the Lydian, it resembles it in a striking manner. We now know, however, that the 'Niobe' of Sipylos owes its origin to Hittite art. On the wall of rock out of which the niche is cut wherein the goddess sits Dr. Dennis discovered a cartouche containing Hittite characters. By tying some ladders together he and I succeeded in ascending to it, and taking paper impressions of the hieroglyphs. Among them is a character which has the meaning of 'king'[1].

How came these characters and these creations of Hittite art in a region so remote from that in which the Hittite kingdoms rose and flourished? How comes it that we find figures of Hittite warriors in the Pass of Karabel and on the rocks of Ghiaur-kalessi, and the image of a Hittite goddess on the cliffs of Sipylos? Whose was the hand that engraved the characters that accompany them,—characters which are the same as those which meet us on the stones of Hamath and Carchemish? We have now to learn what answers can be given to these questions.

[1] A copy of the inscription made from the squeeze is given in the *Transactions of the Society of Biblical Archæology*, VII. Pt. 3, Pl. v. An eye-copy, made from the ground by Dr. Dennis, on the occasion of his discovery of the cartouche, was published in the *Proceedings* of the same Society for January 1881, and is necessarily imperfect.

MONUMENT OF A HITTITE KING FOUND AT CARCHEMISH.

CHAPTER IV.

THE HITTITE EMPIRE.

WE have seen that the Egyptian monuments bear witness to an extension of Hittite power into the distant regions of Asia Minor. When the kings of Kadesh contended with the great Pharaoh of the Oppression they were able to summon to their aid allies from the Troad, as well as from Lydia and the shores of the Cilician sea. A century later Egypt was again invaded by a confederacy, consisting partly of the Hittite rulers of Carchemish and Aleppo, partly of Libyans and Teukrians, and other populations of Asia Minor. If any trust can be placed in the identifications proposed by Egyptian scholars for the countries from whence the vassals and allies of the Hittites came it is clear that memorials of Hittite power and conquest ought to be found in Asia Minor.

And they were found as soon as it was recognised that the curious monuments of Asia Minor, of which the warriors of Karabel and the sculptures of Ibreez are examples, were actually inspired by Hittite art. As soon as it was known that the art these monuments represented, and the peculiar form of writing which accompanied them, had their earliest home in the Syrian cities of the Hittite tribes, a new light broke over the prehistoric past of Asia Minor. These Hittite monuments can be traced in two continuous lines from

Northern Syria and Kappadokia to the western extremity of the peninsula. They follow the two highways
which once led out of Asia to Sardes and the shores of
the Ægean. In the south they form as it were a series
of stations at Ibreez and Bulgar Maden in Lykaonia, at
Fassiler and Tyriaion between Ikonion and the Lake
of Beyshehr, and finally in the Pass of Karabel. Northwards the line runs through the Taurus by Merash,
and carries us first to the defile of Ghurun, and then to
the great Kappadokian ruins of Boghaz Keui and
Eyuk, from whence we pass by Ghiaur-kalessi and the
burial-place of the old Phrygian kings, until we again
reach the Lydian capital and the Pass of Karabel.

Westward of the Halys and Kappadokia they are
marked by certain peculiarities. They are found either
in the vicinity of silver mines, like those of Lykaonia, or
else on the line of the ancient roads, which finally con-
verged in Lydia. None have been discovered in the
central plateau of Asia Minor, in the mountains of
Lykia in the south, or the wide-reaching coast-lands of
the north. They mark the sites of small colonies, or
else the lines of road that connected them. Moreover,
with the exception of the image of the goddess who
sits on her throne in Mount Sipylos, the western monuments represent the figures of warriors who are in the
act of marching forward. This is the case at Karabel;
it is also the case at Ghiaur-kalessi, where the rock on
which the two Hittite warriors are carved lies close
below the remains of a pre-historic fortress.

Such facts admit of only one explanation. The
Hittite monuments of Western Asia Minor must be
memorials of military conquest and supremacy. In the
warriors whose figures stood on either side of the Pass

of Karabel, the sculptor must have seen the visible symbols of Hittite power. They showed that the Hittite had won and kept the pass by force of arms. They are emblems of conquest, not creations of native art.

But it was inevitable that conquest should bring with it a civilising influence. The Hittites could not carry with them the art and culture they had acquired in the East without influencing the barbarous populations over whom they claimed to rule. The vassal chieftains of Lydia and the Troad could not lead their forces into Syria, or assist in the invasion of Egypt, without learning something of that ancient civilisation with which they had come in contact. The Hittites, in fact, must be regarded as the first teachers of the rude populations of the West. They brought to them a culture the first elements of which had been inspired by Babylonia ; they brought also a system of writing out of which, in all probability, the natives of Asia Minor afterwards developed a writing of their own.

It is possible, therefore, that some of the Hittite monuments of Asia Minor are the work, not of the Hittites themselves, but of the native populations whom they had civilised and instructed. It may be that this is the case at Ibreez, where the faces of the god and his worshipper have Jewish features very unlike those found on monuments of purely Hittite origin. But apart from such instances, where the monument is due to Hittite influence rather than to Hittite artists, it is certain that most of the Hittite memorials of Asia Minor are the productions of the Hittites themselves. This is proved by the hieroglyphs which are attached to them, as well as by the uniform type of feature and

dress which prevails from Carchemish to the Ægean.
It is impossible to explain such an uniformity, and still
more the extraordinary resemblance between the
characters engraved at Karabel, or on Mount Sipylos,
and those which meet us in the inscriptions of Hamath
and Carchemish, except on the supposition that the
monuments were executed by men who belonged to the
same race and spoke the same language. Wherever
Hittite inscriptions occur, we find in them the same
combinations of hieroglyphs as well as the use of the
same characters to denote grammatical suffixes.

We may, then, rest satisfied with the conclusion that
the existence of a Hittite empire extending into Asia
Minor is certified, not only by the records of ancient
Egypt, but also by Hittite monuments which still exist.
In the days of Ramses II., when the children of Israel
were groaning under the tasks allotted to them, the
enemies of their oppressors were already exercising a
power and a domination which rivalled that of Egypt.
The Egyptian monarch soon learned to his cost that the
Hittite prince was as 'great' a king as himself, and
could summon to his aid the inhabitants of the unknown
north. Pharaoh's claim to sovereignty was disputed by
adversaries as powerful as the ruler of Egypt, if indeed
not more powerful, and there was always a refuge
among them for those who were oppressed by the
Egyptian king.

When, however, we speak of a Hittite empire we
must understand clearly what that means. It was not
an empire like that of Rome, where the subject provinces
were consolidated together under a central authority,
obeying the same laws and the same supreme head.
It was not an empire like that of the Persians, or of the

Assyrian successors of Tiglath-pileser III., which represented the organised union of numerous states and nations under a single ruler. Such a conception of empire was due to Tiglath-pileser III., and his successor Sargon ; it was a new idea in the world, and had never been realised before. The first Assyrian empire, like the foreign empire of Egypt, was of an altogether different character. It depended on the military enterprise and strength of individual monarchs. As long as the Assyrian or Egyptian king could lead his armies into distant territories, and compel their inhabitants to pay him tribute and homage, his empire extended over them. But hardly had he returned home laden with spoil than we find the subject populations throwing off their allegiance and asserting their independence, while the death of the conqueror brought with it almost invariably the general uprising of the tribes and cities his arms had subdued. Before the days of Tiglath-pileser, in fact, empire in Western Asia meant the power of a prince to force a foreign people to submit to his rule. The conquered provinces had to be subdued again and again ; but as long as this could be done, as long as the native struggles for freedom could be crushed by a campaign, so long did the empire exist.

It was an empire of this sort that the Hittites established in Asia Minor. How long it lasted we cannot say. But so long as the distant races of the West answered the summons to war of the Hittite princes, it remained a reality. The fact that the tribes of the Troad and Lydia are found fighting under the command of the Hittite kings of Kadesh, proves that they acknowledged the supremacy of their Hittite lords, and followed them to battle like the vassals of some feudal chief.

If Hittite armies had not marched to the shores of the
Ægean, and Hittite princes been able from time to time
to exact homage from the nations of the far west,
Egypt would not have had to contend against the
populations of Asia Minor in its wars with the Hittites,
and the figures of Hittite warriors would not have been
sculptured on the rocks of Karabel. There was a time
when the Hittite name was feared as far as the western
extremity of Asia Minor, and when Hittite satraps had
their seat in the future capital of Lydia.

Traditions of this period lingered on into classical
days. The older dynasty of Lydian kings traced its
descent from Bel and Ninos, the Babylonian or Assyrian
gods, whose names had been carried by the Hittites into
the remote west. The Lydian hero Kayster, who gave
his name to the Kaystrian plain, was fabled to have
wandered into Syria, and there, after wooing Semiramis,
to have been the father of Derketo, the goddess of
Carchemish. A Lydian was even said to have drowned
Derketo in the sacred lake of Ashkelon ; and Eusebius
declares that Sardes, the Lydian capital, was captured
for the first time in B.C. 1078, by a horde of invaders
from the north-western regions of Asia.

But it is in the famous legend of the Amazons that
we must look for the chief evidence preserved to us by
classical antiquity of the influence once exercised by the
Hittites in Asia Minor. The Amazons were imagined
to be a nation of female warriors, whose primitive home
lay in Kappadokia, on the banks of the Thermodon, not
far from the ruins of Boghaz Keui. From hence they
had issued forth to conquer the people of Asia Minor
and to found an empire which reached to the Ægean
Sea. The building of many of the most famous cities

on the Ægean coast was ascribed to them,—Myrina and
Kyme, Smyrna and Ephesos, where the worship of the
great Asiatic goddess was carried on with barbaric ceremonies into the later age of civilised Greece.

Now these Amazons are nothing more than the
priestesses of the Asiatic goddess, whose cult spread
from Carchemish along with the advance of the Hittite
armies. She was served by a multitude of armed priestesses and eunuch priests ; under her name of Ma, for
instance, no less than six thousand of them waited on
her at Komana in Kappadokia. Certain cities, in fact,
like Komana and Ephesos, were dedicated to her service,
and a large part of the population accordingly became
the armed ministers of the mighty goddess. Generally
these were women, as at Ephesos in early days, where
they obeyed a high-priestess, who called herself 'the
queen-bee.' When Ephesos passed into Greek hands,
the goddess worshipped there was identified with the
Greek Artemis, and a high-priest took the place of the
high-priestess. But the priestess of Artemis still continued to be called 'a bee,' reminding us that Deborah
or 'Bee' was the name of one of the greatest of the
prophetesses of ancient Israel; and the goddess herself
continued to be depicted under the same form as that
which had belonged to her in Hittite days. On her
head was the so-called mural crown, the Hittite origin
of which has now been placed beyond doubt by the
sculptures of Boghaz Keui, while her chariot was drawn
by lions. It was from the Hittites, too, that Artemis
received her sacred animal, the goat.

The 'spear-armed host' of the Amazons, which came
from Kappadokia, which conquered Asia Minor, and was
so closely connected with the worship of the Ephesian

Artemis, can be no other than the priestesses of the Hittite goddess, who danced in her honour armed with the shield and bow. In ancient art the Amazons are represented as clad in the Hittite tunic and brandishing the same double-headed axe that is held in the hands of some of the Hittite deities on the rocks of Boghaz Keui, while the 'spear' lent to them by the Greek poet brings to our recollection the spear held by the warriors of Karabel. We cannot explain the myth of the Amazons except on the supposition that they represented the armed priestesses of the Hittite goddess, and that a tradition of the Hittite empire in Asia Minor has entwined itself around the story of their arrival in the West. The cities they are said to have founded must have been the seats of Hittite rule.

The Hittites were intruders in Syria as well as in Western Asia Minor. Everything points to the conclusion that they had descended from the ranges of the Taurus. Their costume was that of the inhabitants of a cold and mountainous region, not of the warm valleys of the south. In place of the trailing robes of the Syrians, the national costume was a tunic which did not quite reach to the knees. It was only after their settlement in the Syrian cities that they adopted the dress of the country ; the sculptured rocks of Asia Minor represent them with the same short tunic as that which distinguished the Dorians of Greece or the ancient inhabitants of Ararat. But the most characteristic portion of the Hittite garb were the shoes with upturned ends. Wherever the figure of a Hittite is portrayed, there we find this peculiar form of boot. It reappears among the hieroglyphs of the inscriptions, and the Egyptian artists who adorned the walls of the Ramesscum at Thebes have placed it on the feet of the Hittite defenders of Kadesh. The boot is really a snow-shoe, admirably adapted for walking over snow, but ill-suited for the inhabitants of a level or cultivated country. The fact that it was still used by the Hittites of Kadesh in the warm fertile valley of the Orontes proves better than any other argument that they must have come from the snow-clad mountains of the north. It is like the shoe of similar shape which the Turks have carried with them in their migrations from the north and introduced amongst the natives of Syria and Egypt. It indicates with unerring certainty the northern origin of the Turkish conqueror. He stands in the same relation to the modern population of Syria that the Hittites stood to the Arameans of Kadesh three thousand years ago.

Equally significant is the long fingerless glove which is one of the most frequent of Hittite hieroglyphs. The thumb alone is detached from the rest of the bag in which the fingers were enclosed. Such a glove is an eloquent witness to the wintry cold of the regions from which its wearers came, and a similar glove is still used during the winter months by the peasants of modern Kappadokia.

We may find another evidence of the northern descent of the Hittite tribes in the hieroglyph which is used in the sense of 'country.' It represents two, or sometimes three, pointed mountains, whose forms, as was remarked some years ago, resemble those of the mountains about Kaisariyeh, the Kappadokian capital.

If we leave Kadesh and proceed northwards, the local names bear more and more the peculiar stamp of a Hittite origin. We leave Semitic names like

F

Kadesh, 'the sanctuary,' behind us, and at length find ourselves in a district where the geographical names no longer admit of a Semitic etymology. It is just this district, moreover, in which Hittite inscriptions first become plentiful. The first met with to the south are the stones of Hamath and the lost inscription of Aleppo ; but from Carchemish northwards we now know that numbers of them still exist. The territory covered by them is a square, the base of which is formed by a line running from Carchemish through Antioch into Lykaonia, while the remains at Boghaz Keui and Eyuk constitute its northern limit. We must regard this region as having been the primeval home and starting-point of the Hittite race. They will have been a population which clustered round the two flanks of the Taurus range, extending far into Kappadokia on the north, and towards Armenia on the east.

They preserved their independence on the banks of the Halys in Kappadokia for nearly two hundred years after the fall of Carchemish. It was not long before the overthrow of Lydia by Cyrus that Krœsos, the Lydian king, destroyed the cities of Pteria, where the ruins of Boghaz Keui and Eyuk now stand, and enslaved their inhabitants, thus avenging upon them the conquest of his own country by their ancestors so many centuries before. Herodotos calls them ' Syrians,' a name which is qualified as ' White Syrians ' by the Greek geographer Strabo. It was in this way that the Greek writer wished to distinguish them from the dark-coloured Syrians of Aramean or Jewish birth, with whom he was otherwise acquainted ; and it reminds us that, whereas the Egyptian artists painted the Hittites with yellow skins, they painted the Syrians

THE DOUBLE-HEADED EAGLE OF EYUK.

with red. It is an interesting fact that the memory
of their relationship to the population on the Syrian
side of the Taurus should have been preserved so long
among these Hittites of Kappadokia.

Boghaz Keui and Eyuk are situated in the district
known as Pteria to the Greeks. At Eyuk there are
remains of a vast palace, which stood on an artificial
platform of earth, like the palaces of Assyria and
Babylon. The walls of the palace, formed of huge
blocks of cut stone, can still be traced in many places.
It was approached by an avenue of sculptured slabs,
on which lions were represented, some of them in the
act of devouring a ram. The head and attitude of
one that is preserved remind us of the avenue of ram-
headed sphinxes which led to the temple of Karnak
at Thebes. The entrance of the palace was flanked
on either side by two enormous monoliths of granite,
on the external faces of which were carved in relief the
images of a sphinx. But though the artist had clearly
gone to Egypt for his model, it is also clear that he
had modified the forms he imitated in accordance with
national ideas. The head-dress, like the feet, of the
sphinxes is non-Egyptian, the necklace passes under
the chin instead of falling across the breast, and the
sphinx itself is erect, not recumbent, as in Egypt. On
the right hand the same block of stone which bears
the figure of the sphinx bears also, on the inner side,
the figure of a double-headed eagle, with an animal
which Professor Perrot believes to be a hare in either
talon, and a man standing upon its twofold head.
The same double-headed eagle, supporting the figure
of a man or a god, is met with at Boghaz Keui, and
must be regarded as one of the peculiarities of Hittite

symbolism and art. The symbol was adopted in later days by the Turkoman princes, who had perhaps first seen it on the Hittite monuments of Kappodokia; and the Crusaders brought it to Europe with them in the 14th century. Here it became the emblem of the German Emperors, who have passed it on to the modern kingdoms of Russia and Austria. It is not the only heir-loom of Hittite art which has descended to us of to-day.

The lintel of the palace gate at Eyuk was of solid stone, and, if Professor Perrot is right, the huge stone lintel, adorned with a lion's head, still lies in fragments on the ground. The entrance was flanked with walls on which bas-reliefs were carved, as in the palaces which were built by the kings of Assyria. They formed, in fact, a dado, the rest of the wall above them being probably of brick covered with stucco and painted with bright colours. Many of the sculptured blocks still lie scattered on the ground. Here we have the picture of a priest before an altar, there of a sacred bull mounted on a pedestal. Hard by is the likeness of two men, one of whom carries a lyre, the other a goat; while on another stone a man is represented with little regard to perspective in the act of climbing a ladder. Another relief introduces to us three rams and a goat whose horn is grasped by a shepherd; elsewhere again we see a goddess seated in a chair of peculiar construction, with her feet upon a stool and objects like flowers in her hand. A similar piece of sculpture has been found at Merash, on the southern side of the Taurus, within the limits of the ancient Komagene, even such details as the form of the chair and stool being alike in the two cases. The two reliefs might have been executed by the same hand.

The sphinxes which guarded the entrance of the palace of Eyuk and the avenue which led up to them bear unmistakable testimony to the influence of Egyptian art upon its builders. They take us back to a period when the Hittites of Kappadokia were in contact with the people of the Nile, and thus confirm the evidence of the Egyptian records. There must have been a time when the population of distant Kappadokia held intercourse with that of Egypt, and this time, as we learn from the Egyptian monuments, was the age of Ramses II. It is perhaps not going too far to assume that the palace of Eyuk was erected in the 13th century before our era, and is a relic of the period when the sway of the Hittite princes of Kadesh or Carchemish extended as far north as the neighbourhood of the Halys. It is indeed possible that the palace was originally the summer residence of the kings whose homes were in the south. The plateau on which Eyuk and Boghaz Keui stand is more than 2000 feet above the level of the sea, and the winters there are intensely cold. From December onwards the ground is piled high with snow. It is well known that the descendants of races which have originally come from a cold climate endure the heats of a southern summer with impatience ; and the same causes which make the English rulers of India to-day retire during the summer to the mountain heights, may have made the Hittite lords of Syria build their summer palace in the Kappadokian highlands.

The sculptures of Boghaz Keui belong to a somewhat later date than those of Eyuk. Boghaz Keui is five hours to the south-west of Eyuk, and marks the site of a once populous town. A stream that runs past

it separates the ruins of the city from a remarkable
series of sculptures carved on the rocks of the mountains
which overlooked the city.   The city was surrounded

SCULPTURES AT BOGHAZ KEUI.

by a massive wall of masonry, and within it were two
citadels solidly built on the summits of two shafts of

rock. The wall was without towers, but at its foot ran a moat cut partly through the rock, partly through the earth. the earth being coated with a smooth and slippery covering of masonry. The most important building in the city was the palace, a plan of which has been made by modern travellers. Like the palace of Eyuk, it was erected on an artificial mound or terrace of earth, and its ornamentation seems to have been similar to that of Eyuk. But little is left of it save the foundations of the walls and the overturned throne of stone which once stood in the central court supported on the bodies of two lions. Lions' heads were also carved on the columns which formed the door-posts of the city-gate.

The interest of Boghaz Keui centres in the sculptures which have been carved with so much care on the rocky walls of the mountains. Here advantage has been taken of two narrow recesses, the sides and floors of which have been artificially shaped and levelled. The first and largest recess may be described as of rectangular shape. Along either side of it, as along the dado of a room, run two long lines of figures in relief, which eventually meet at the end opposite the entrance. On the left-hand side we see a line of men, almost all clad alike in the short tunic, peaked tiara, and boots with upturned ends that characterise Hittite art. At times, however, they are interrupted by other figures in the long Syrian robe, who may perhaps be intended for women. Among them are two dwarf-like creatures upholding the crescent disk of the moon, and after a while the procession becomes that of a number of deities, each with his name written in Hittite hieroglyphs at his side. After turning the corner of the recess, the procession consists of three gods, two of whom stand on mountain-peaks, while the foremost (with a goat beside him) is supported on the heads of two adoring priests. Facing him is the foremost figure of the other procession, which starts from the eastern side of the recess, and finally meets the first on its northern wall. This figure is that of the great Asiatic goddess, who wears on her head the mural crown and stands upon a panther, while beside her, as beside the god she is greeting, is the portraiture of a goat. Behind her a youthful god, with the double-headed battle-axe in his hand, stands upon a panther, and behind him again are two priestesses with mural crowns, whose feet rest upon the heads and wings of a double-headed eagle. This eagle, whose form is but a reproduction of that sculptured at Eyuk, closes the series of designs represented on the northern wall. The eastern wall is occupied with a long line, first of goddesses and then of priestesses. Where the line breaks off at last we come upon a solitary piece of sculpture. This is the image of an eunuch-priest, who stands on a mountain and holds in one hand a curved augural wand, in the other a strange symbol representing a priest with embroidered robes, who stands upon a shoe with upturned ends, and supports a winged solar disk, the two extremities of which rest upon baseless columns.

The entrance to the second recess is guarded on either side by two winged monsters, with human bodies and the heads of dogs. It leads into an artificially excavated passage of rectangular shape, on the rocky walls of which detached groups of figures and emblems are engraved. On the western wall is a row of twelve priests or soldiers, each of whom bears a scythe upon

SCULPTURES AT BOGHAZ KEUI.

his shoulder; facing them on the eastern wall are two reliefs of strange character. One of them depicts the youthful god, whose name perhaps was Attys, embracing with his left arm the eunuch-priest, above whose head is engraved the strange symbol that has been already described. The other represents a god's head crowned with the peaked tiara, and supported on a double-headed lion, which again stands on the hinder feet of two other lions, whose heads rest on a column or stem. All these sculptures were once covered with stucco, and thus preserved from the action of the weather.

It is evident that in these two mountain recesses we have a sanctuary, the forms and symbols of whose deities were sculptured on its walls of living rock. It was a sanctuary too holy to be confined within the walls of the city, and the supreme deities to whom it was dedicated were a god and a goddess, served by a multitude of male and female priests. In fact, as Prof. Perrot remarks, Boghaz Keui must have been a sacred city like Komana, whose citizens were consecrated to the chief divinities adored by the Hittites, and were governed by a high-priest. It was as much a 'Kadesh' or 'Hierapolis,' as much a 'holy city,' as Carchemish itself.

It is not its sculptures only which prove to us that it was a city of the Hittites. The figures of the deities have attached to them, as at Eyuk, the same hieroglyphs as those which meet us in the inscriptions of Hamath and Aleppo, of Carchemish and Merash, and within its walls, southward of the ruins of its palace, Prof. Perrot discovered a long text of nine or ten lines cut out of the rock, and though worn and disfigured by time and weather, still showing the forms of many

Hittite characters. So far as can be judged from a photograph of it he has published, the forms are the same as those which are found on the Hittite monuments of Syria.

Tedious as all these details may seem to be, it has been necessary to give them, since they tell us what was the appearance and construction of a Hittite city, a Hittite palace, and the interior of a Hittite temple. The discoveries recently made in the Hittite districts south of the Taurus, show us that here too the palaces and temples were like those of Eyuk and Boghaz Keui. Here too we find the same dados sculptured with the same figures dressed in the same costume ; here too we meet with the same lions, and the same winged deities standing on the backs of animals. A photograph of a piece of sculpture on a block of basalt at Carchemish, taken by Dr. Gwyther, might have been taken at Boghaz Keui. The art, the forms, and the symbolism are all the same.

The high-road from Boghaz Keui to Merash must have passed through the defile of Ghurun, where Sir Charles Wilson discovered Hittite inscriptions carved upon the cliff. But there may have been a second road which led through Kaisariyeh, the modern capital of Kappadokia, southward to Bor or Tyana, where Prof. Ramsay found a Hittite text, and from thence to the silver mines of the Bulgar Dagh. The bas-reliefs of Ibreez are not far distant from the famous Cilician gates which led the traveller from the great central plateau of Asia Minor to Tarsus and the sea.

It would seem that the silver mines of the Bulgar Dagh were first worked by Hittite miners. Silver had a special attraction for the Hittite race. The material on which the Hittite version of the treaty between the Hittite king of Kadesh and the Egyptian Pharaoh was written was a tablet of that metal. That such tablets were in frequent use, results from the fact that nearly all the Hittite inscriptions known to us are not incised, but cut in relief upon the stone. It is therefore obvious that the Hittites must have first inscribed their hieroglyphs upon metal, rather than upon wood or stone or clay; it is only in the case of metal that it is less laborious to hammer or cast in relief than to cut the metal with a graving tool, and nothing can prove more clearly how long accustomed the Hittite scribes must have been to doing so, than their imitation of this work in relief when they came to write upon stone. It is possible that most of the silver of which they made use came from the Bulgar Dagh. The Hittite inscription found near the old mines of these mountains by Mr. Davis, proves that they had once occupied the locality. It is even possible that their settlement for a time in Lydia was also connected with their passion for 'the bright metal.' At all events the Gumush Dagh, or 'Silver Mountains,' lie to the south of the Pass of Karabel, and traces of old workings can still be detected in them.

However this may be, the Hittite monuments of Asia Minor confirm in a striking way the evidence of the Egyptian inscriptions. They show us that the Hittites worked for silver in the mountains which looked down upon the Cilician plain, from whence the influence of their art and writing extended into the plain itself. They further show that the central point of Hittite power was a square on either side of the Taurus range, which included Carchemish and Komagene in the south, the district eastwards of the Halys on the north, and the country of which Malatiyeh was the capital in the east. The Hittite tribes, in fact, were mountaineers from the plateau of Kappadokia who had spread themselves out in all directions. A time came when, under the leadership of powerful princes, they marched along the two high-roads of Asia Minor and established their supremacy over the coast-tribes of the far west. The age to which this military empire belongs is indicated by the Egyptian character of the so-called image of Niobe on the cliff of Sipylos, as well as by the sphinxes which guarded the entrance to the palace of Eyuk. It goes back to the days when the rulers of Kadesh could summon to their aid the vassal-chieftains of the Ægean coast. The monuments the Hittites have left behind them in Asia Minor thus bear the same testimony as the records of Egypt. The people to whom Uriah, and it may be Bath-sheba, belonged, not only had contended on equal terms with one of the greatest of Egyptian kings ; they had carried their arms through the whole length of Asia Minor, they had set up satraps in the cities of Lydia, and had brought the civilisation of the East to the barbarous tribes of the distant West.

CHAPTER V.

THE HITTITE CITIES AND RACE.

OF the history of the 'White Syrians' or Hittites who lived in the land of Pteria, near the Halys, we know nothing at present beyond what we can gather from the ruins of their stronghold at Boghaz Keui and their palace at Eyuk. The same is the case with the Hittite tribes of Malatiyeh and Komagene. When the inscription which adorns the body of a stone lion found at Merash can be deciphered, it will doubtless cast light on the early history of the city ; at present we do not know even its ancient name. It is not until we leave the mountainous region originally occupied by the Hittite race, and descend into the valleys of Syria, that the annals of their neighbours begin to tell us something about their fortunes and achievements. The history of their two southern capitals, Carchemish and Kadesh, broken and imperfect though it may be, is not an utter blank.

The site of Carchemish had long been looked for in vain. At one time it was identified with the Kirkesion or Circesium of classical geography, built at the confluence of the Khabour and the Euphrates. But the Assyrian name of Kirkesion was Sirki, and its position did not agree with that assigned to 'Gargamis' or Carchemish in the Assyrian texts. Professor Maspero subsequently placed the latter at Membij, the ancient Mabog or Hierapolis, on the strength of the evidence furnished by

G

classical authors and the Egyptian monuments; but the ruins of Membij contain nothing earlier than the Greek period, and their position on a rocky plateau at a distance from the Euphrates, is inconsistent with the fact known to us from the Assyrian inscriptions, that Carchemish commanded the fords over the Euphrates.

To Mr. Skene, for many years the English consul at Aleppo, is due the credit of first discovering the true site of the old Hittite capital. On the western bank of the Euphrates, midway between Birejik and the mouth of the Sajur, rises an artificial mound of earth, under which ruins and sculptured blocks of stone had been found from time to time. It was known as Jerablus, or Kalaat Jerablus, 'the fortress of Jerablus,' sometimes wrongly written Jerabîs; and in the name of Jerablus Mr. Skene had no difficulty in recognising an Arab corruption of Hierapolis. In the Roman age the name of Hierapolis or 'Holy City' had been transferred to its neighbour Membij, which inherited the traditions and religious fame of the older Carchemish; but when the triumph of Christianity in Syria brought with it the fall of the great temple of Membij, the name disappeared from the later city, and was remembered only in connection with the ruins of the ancient Carchemish.

Two years after Mr. Skene's discovery, Mr. George Smith visited Carchemish on his last ill-fated journey from which he never returned, and recognised at once that Mr. Skene's identification was right. The position of Jerablus suited the requirements of the Assyrian texts, it lay on the high-road which formerly led from east to west, and among its ruins was an inscription in Hittite characters. Not long afterwards there were brought to the British Museum the bronze bands which once adorned the gates of an Assyrian temple, and on one of these is a picture in relief of Carchemish as it looked in the days of Jehu of Israel. The Euphrates is represented as running past its walls, thus conclusively showing that Jerablus, and not Membij, must be the site on which it stood.

The site was bought by Mr. Henderson, Mr. Skene's successor at Aleppo, and the money was invested by the former owner in the purchase of a cow. The mighty were fallen indeed, when the Hittite capital which had resisted the armies of Egypt and Assyria was judged to be worth no more than the price of a beast of the field. In 1878 Mr. Henderson was employed by the Trustees of the British Museum in excavating on the spot; but no sufficient supervision was exercised over the workmen, and though a few remains of Hittite sculpture and writing found their way to London, much was left to be burned into lime by the natives or employed in the construction of a mill.

The ancient city was defended on two sides by the Euphrates, and was exposed only on the north and west. Here, however, an artificial canal had been cut, on either side of which was a fortified wall. The mound which had first attracted Mr. Skene's attention marks the site of the royal palace, where the excavators found the remains of a dado like that of Eyuk, the face of the stones having been sculptured into the likeness of gods and men. The men were shod with boots with upturned ends, that unfailing characteristic of Hittite art.

Carchemish enjoyed a long history. When first we hear of it in the Egyptian records it was already in Hittite hands. Thothmes III. fought beneath its walls, and his bravest warriors plunged into the Euphrates in their eagerness to capture the foe. Tiglath-pileser I. had seen its walls from the opposite shore of the Euphrates, but had not ventured to approach them. Assurnatsir-pal and his son Shalmaneser had received tribute from its king, and when it finally surrendered to the armies of Sargon it was made the seat of an Assyrian satrap. The trade which had flowed through it continued to pour wealth into the hands of its merchants, and the 'maneh of Carchemish' remained a standard of value. When Egypt made her final struggle for supremacy in Asia, it was under the walls of Carchemish that the decisive struggle was fought. The battle of Carchemish in B.C. 604 drove Necho out of Syria and Palestine, and placed the destinies of the chosen people in the hands of the Babylonian king. It is possible that the ruin of Carchemish dates from the battle. However that may be, long before the beginning of the Christian era it had been supplanted by Mabog or Membij, and the great sanctuary which had made it a 'holy city' was transferred to its rival and successor.

Like Carchemish, Kadesh on the Orontes, the most southern capital the Hittites possessed, was also a 'holy city.' Pictures of it have been preserved on the monuments of Ramses II. We gather from them that it stood on the shore of the Lake of Homs, still called the 'Lake of Kadesh,' at the point where the Orontes flowed out of the lake. The river was conducted round the city in a double channel, across which a wide bridge was thrown, the space between the two channels being apparently occupied by a wall.

Kadesh must have been one of the last conquests made by the Hittites in Syria, and their retention of it was the visible sign of their supremacy over Western

Asia. We do not know when they were forced to yield up its possession to others. As has been pointed out, the correct reading of 2 Sam. xxiv. 6 informs us that the northern limit of the kingdom of David was formed by 'the Hittites of Kadesh,' 'the entering in of Hamath,' as it seems to be called elsewhere. In the age of David, accordingly, Kadesh must still have been in their hands, but it had already ceased to be so when the Assyrian king Shalmaneser III. led his armies to the west. No allusion to the city and its inhabitants occurs in the Assyrian inscriptions, and we may conjecture that it had been destroyed by the Syrians of Damascus. As Membij took the place of Carchemish, so Emesa or Homs took the place of Kadesh.

We have seen that the Hittites were a northern race. Their primitive home probably lay on the northern side of the Taurus. What they were like we can learn both from their own sculptures and from the Egyptian monu- ments, which agree most remarkably in the delineation of their features. The extraordinary resemblance be- tween the Hittite faces drawn by the Egyptian artists and those depicted by themselves in their bas-reliefs and their hieroglyphs, is a convincing proof of the faith- fulness of the Egyptian representations, as well as of the identity of the Hittites of the Egyptian inscriptions with the Hittites of Carchemish and Kappadokia.

It must be confessed that they were not a handsome people. They were short and thick of limb, and the front part of their faces was pushed forward in a curious and somewhat repulsive way. The forehead retreated, the cheek-bones were high, the nostrils were large, the upper lip protrusive. They had, in fact, according to the craniologists, the characteristics of a Mongoloid race.

Like the Mongols, moreover, their skins were yellow
and their eyes and hair were black. They arranged the
hair in the form of a 'pig-tail,' which characterises them
on their own and the Egyptian monuments quite as
much as their snow-shoes with upturned toes.

In Syria they doubtless mixed with the Semitic race,
and the further south they advanced the more likely
they were to become absorbed into the native population. The Hittites of Southern Judah have Semitic
names, and probably spoke a Semitic language. Kadesh
continued to bear to the last its Semitic title, and among
the Hittite names which occur further north there are
several which display a Semitic stamp. In the neighbourhood of Carchemish Hittites and Arameans were
mingled together, and Pethor was at once a Hittite
and an Aramean town. In short, the Hittites in Syria
were like a conquering race everywhere; they formed
merely the governing and upper class, which became
smaller and smaller the further removed they were from
their original seats. Like the Normans in Sicily or the
Etruscans in ancient Italy, they tended gradually to
disappear or else to be absorbed into the subject race.
It was only in their primitive homes that they survived
in their original strength and purity, and though even
in Kappadokia they lost their old languages, adopting
in place of them first Aramaic, then Greek, and lastly
Turkish, we may still observe their features and characteristics in the modern inhabitants of the Taurus
range. Even in certain districts of Kappadokia their
descendants may still be met with. 'The type,' says
Sir Charles Wilson, 'which is not a beautiful one, is still
found in some parts of Kappadokia, especially amongst
the people living in the extraordinary subterranean

towns which I discovered beneath the great plain north-west of Nigdeh.' The characteristics of race, when once acquired, seem almost indelible ; and it is possible that, when careful observations can be made, it will be found that the ancient Hittite race still survives, not only in Eastern Asia Minor, but even in the southern regions of Palestine.

CHAPTER VI.

HITTITE RELIGION AND ART.

LUCIAN, or some other Greek writer who has usurped his name, has left us a minute account of the great temple of Mabog as it existed in the second century of the Christian era. Mabog, as we have seen, was the successor of Carchemish; and there is little reason to doubt that the pagan temple of Mabog, with all the rites and ceremonies that were carried on in it, differed but little from the pagan temple of the older Carchemish.

It stood, we are told, in the very centre of the 'Holy City.' It consisted of an outer court and an inner sanctuary, which again contained a Holy of Holies, entered only by the high-priest and those of his companions who were 'nearest the gods.' The temple was erected on an artificial mound or platform, more than twelve feet in height, and its walls and ceiling within were brilliant with gold. Its doors were also gilded, but the Holy of Holies or innermost shrine was not provided with doors, being separated from the rest of the building, it would seem, like the Holy of Holies in the Jewish temple, by a curtain or veil. On either side of the entrance was a cone-like column of great height, a symbol of the goddess of fertility, and in the outer court a large altar of brass. To the left of the latter was an image of 'Semiramis,' and not far off a great 'sea' or 'lake,' containing sacred fish. Oxen, horses, eagles, bears, and lions were kept in the court, as being sacred to the deities worshipped within.

On entering the temple the visitor saw on his left the throne of the Sun-god, but no image, since the Sun and Moon alone of the gods had no images dedicated to them. Beyond, however, were the statues of various divinities, among others the wonder-working image of a god who was believed to deliver oracles and prophecies. At times, it was said, the image moved of its own accord, and if not lifted up at once by the priests, began to perspire. When the priests took it in their hands, it led them from one part of the temple to the other, until the high-priest, standing before it, asked it questions, which it answered by driving its bearers forward. The central objects of worship, however, were the golden images of two deities, whom Lucian identifies with the Greek Hera and Zeus, another figure standing between them, on the head of which rested a golden dove. The goddess, who blazed with precious stones, bore in her hand a sceptre and on her head that turreted or mural crown which distinguishes the goddesses of Boghaz Keui. Like them, moreover, she was supported on lions, while her consort was carried by bulls. In him we may recognise the god who at Boghaz Keui is advancing to meet the supreme Hittite goddess.

In the Egyptian text of the treaty between Ramses and the king of Kadesh, the supreme Hittite god is called Sutekh, the goddess being Antarata, or perhaps Astarata. In later days, however, the goddess of Carchemish was known as Athar-'Ati, which the Greeks transformed into Atargatis and Derketo. Derketo was fabled to be the mother of Semiramis, in whom Greek legend saw an Assyrian queen ; but Semiramis was really the goddess Istar, called Ashtoreth in Canaan, and Atthar or Athar by the Arameans, among whom Carchemish was built. Derketo was, therefore, but another form of Semiramis, or rather but another name under which the great Asiatic goddess was known. The dove was sacred to her, and this explains why an image of the dove was placed above the head of the third image in the divine triad of Mabog.

The temple was served by a multitude of priests. More than 300 took part in the sacrifices on the day when Lucian saw it. The priests were dressed in white, and wore the skull-cap which we find depicted on the Hittite monuments. The high-priest alone carried on his head the lofty tiara, which the sculptures indicate was a prerogative of gods and kings. Prominent among the priests were the Galli or eunuchs, who on the days of festival cut their arms and scourged themselves in honour of their deities. Such actions remind us of those priests of Baal who 'cut themselves after their manner with knives and lancets, till the blood gushed out upon them.'

Twice a year a solemn procession took place to a small chasm in the rock under the temple, where, it was alleged, the waters of the deluge had been swallowed up, and water from the sea was poured into it. It is to this pit that Melito, a Christian writer of Syria, alludes when he says that the goddess Simi, the daughter of the supreme god Hadad, put an end to the attacks of a demon by filling with sea water the pit in which he lived. But in Lucian's time the demon was regarded as the deluge, and the account of the deluge given to the Greek writer agrees so closely with that which we read in Genesis as to make it clear that it had been borrowed by the priests of Hierapolis from the Hebrew Scriptures. It is probable, however, that the tradition itself was of much older standing, and had originally been imported from Babylonia. At all events the hero of the deluge was called Sisythes, a modification of the name of the Chaldæan Noah, while Major Conder found a place in the close neighbourhood of Kadesh which is known as 'the Ark of the Prophet Noah,' and close at hand a spring termed the Tannur or 'Oven,' out of which, according to Mohammedan belief, the waters of the flood gushed forth.

But there were many other festivals at Mabog besides that which commemorated the subsidence of the deluge. Pilgrims flocked to it from all parts—Arabia, Palestine, Kappadokia, Babylonia, even India. They were required to drink water only, and to sleep on the ground. Numerous and rich were the offerings which they brought to the shrine, and once arrived there were called upon to offer sacrifices. Goats and sheep were the most common victims, though oxen were also offered. The only animal whose flesh was forbidden to be either sacrificed or eaten was the swine; as among the Jews, it was regarded as unclean. After being dedicated in the court of the temple the animal was usually led to the house of the offerer, and there put to death; sometimes, however, it was killed by being thrown from the entrance to the temple. Even children were sacrificed by their parents in this way, after first being tied up in skins and told that they were 'not children but oxen.'

Different stories were current as to the foundation of the temple. There were some who affirmed that

Sisythes had built it after the deluge over the spot
where the waters of the flood had been swallowed up by
the earth. It is possible that this was the legend
originally believed in Mabog before the traditions of
Carchemish had been transferred to it. It seems to be
closely connected with the local peculiarities of the site.
The other legends had doubtless had their origin in the
older Hierapolis. According to one of them, the temple
had been founded by Semiramis in honour of her
mother Derketo, half woman and half fish, to whom the
fish in the neighbouring lake were sacred. Another
account made Attys its founder, and the goddess to whom
it was dedicated the divinity called Rhea by the Greeks.

Derketo and Rhea, however, are but different names
of the same deity, who was known as Kybele or Kybebe
in Phrygia, and honoured with the title of 'the Great
Mother.' Her images were covered with breasts, to
symbolise that she was but mother-earth, from whom
mankind derived their means of life. Her attributes
were borrowed from those of the Babylonian Istar, the
Ashtoreth of Canaan ; even the form assigned to her
was that of the Babylonian Istar, as we learn from a
bas-relief discovered at Carchemish, where she is represented as naked, a lofty tiara alone excepted, with the
hands upon the breasts and a wing rising behind each
shoulder. She was, in fact, a striking illustration of the
influence exerted upon the Hittites, and through them
upon the people of Asia Minor, by Babylonian religion
and worship. Even in Lydia a stone has been found
on which her image is carved in a rude style of art, but
similar in form to the representations of her in the bas-
relief of Carchemish and the cylinders of ancient
Chaldæa.

This stone, like the seated figure on Mount Sipylos, is a witness that her cult was carried westward by the Hittite armies. Later tradition preserved a reminiscence of the fact. The Lydian hero Kayster was said to have gone to Syria, and there had Derketo for his bride, while on the other hand it was a Lydian, Mopsos, who was believed to have drowned the goddess Derketo in the sacred lake of Ashkelon. We have here, it may be, recollections of the days when Lydian soldiers marched against Egypt under the leadership of Hittite princes, and learnt to know the name and the character of Athar-'Ati, the goddess of Carchemish.

The Babylonian Istar was accompanied by her son and bridegroom Tammuz, the youthful Sun-god, the story of whose untimely death made a deep impression on the popular mind. Even in Jerusalem Ezekiel saw the women weeping for the death of Tammuz within the precincts of the temple itself ; and for days together each year in the Phœnician cities the festival of his death and resurrection were observed with fanatic zeal. In Syria he was called Hadad, and identified with the god Rimmon, so that Zechariah (xii. 11) speaks of the mourning for Hadad-Rimmon in the valley of Megiddo. At Hierapolis and Aleppo also he was known as Hadad or Dadi, while throughout Asia Minor he was adored under the name of Attys, 'the shepherd of the bright stars.' The myth which told of his death underwent a slight change of form among the Hittites, and through them among the tribes of Asia Minor. He is doubtless the young god who on the rocks of Boghaz Keui appears behind the mother-goddess, riding like her on the back of a panther or lion.

The people of Mabog did not forget that their temple

was but the successor of an older one, and that Carchemish had once been the ' Holy City' of Northern Syria. The legends, therefore, which referred to the foundation of the sanctuary were said to relate to one which had formerly existed, but had long since fallen into decay. The origin of the temple visited by Lucian was ascribed to a certain ' Stratonike, the wife of the Assyrian king.' But Stratonike is merely a Greek transformation of some Semitic epithet of ' Ashtoreth,' and marks the time when the Phœnician Ashtoreth took the place of the earlier Athar-'Ati. A strange legend was told of the youthful Kombabos, who was sent from Babylon to take part in the building of the shrine. Kombabos was but Tammuz under another name, just as Stratonike was Istar, and the legend is chiefly interesting as testifying to the religious influence once exercised by the Babylonians upon the Hittite people.

Semiramis may turn out to have been the Hittite name of the goddess called Athar-'Ati by the Aramean inhabitants of Hierapolis. In this case the difficulty of accounting for the existence of the two names would have been solved in the old myths by making her the daughter of Derketo. But while Derketo was a fish-goddess, Semiramis was associated with the dove, like the Ashtoreth or Aphrodite who was worshipped in Cyprus. The symbol of the dove had been carried to the distant West at an early period. Among the objects found by Dr. Schliemann in the prehistoric tombs of Mykenæ were figures in gold-leaf, two of which represented a naked goddess with the hands upon the breasts and doves above her, while the third has the form of a temple, on the two pinnacles of which are seated two doves. Considering how intimately the prehistoric art of My-

kenæ seems to have been connected with that of Asia
Minor, it is hardly too much to suppose that the symbol
of the dove had made its way across the Ægean through
the help of the Hittites, and that in the pinnacled temple
of Mykenæ, with its two doves, we may see a picture of
a Hittite temple in Lydia or Kappadokia.

The legends reported by Lucian about the foundation
of the temple of Mabog all agreed that it was dedicated
to a goddess. The 'Holy City' was under the protection,
not of a male but of a female divinity, which explains why
it was that it was served by eunuch priests. If Attys
or Hadad was worshipped there, it was in right of his
mother ; the images of the other gods stood in the
temple on sufferance only. The male deity whom the
Greek author identified with Zeus must have been
regarded as admitted by treaty or marriage to share
in the honours paid to her. It must have been the
same also at Boghaz Keui. Here, too, the most prominent figure in the divine procession is that of the
Mother-goddess, who is followed by her son Attys, while
the god, whose name may be read Tar or Tarku, 'the
king,' and who is the Zeus of Lucian, advances to meet
her.

In Cilicia and Lydia this latter god seems to have
been known as Sandan. He is called on coins the
'Baal of Tarsos,' and he carries in his hand a bunch
of grapes and a stalk of corn. We may see his figure
engraved on the rock of Ibreez. Here he wears on his
head the pointed Hittite cap, ornamented with horn-
like ribbons, besides the short tunic and boots with
upturned ends. On his wrists are bracelets, and ear-
rings hang from his ears.

Sandan was identified with the Sun, and hence it

happened that when a Semitic language came to prevail in Cilicia he was transformed into a supreme Baal. The same transformation had taken place centuries before in the Hittite cities of Syria. Beside the Syrian goddess Kes, who is represented as standing upon a lion, like the great goddess of Carchemish, the Egyptian monuments tell us of Sutekh, who stands in the same relation to his Hittite worshippers as the Semitic Baal stood to the populations of Canaan. Sutekh was the supreme Hittite god, but at the same time he was localised in every city or state in which the Hittites lived. Thus there was a Sutekh of Carchemish and a Sutekh of Kadesh, just as there was a Baal of Tyre and a Baal of Tarsos. The forms under which he was worshipped were manifold, but everywhere it was the same Sutekh, the same national god.

It would seem that the power of Sutekh began to wane after the age of Ramses, and that the goddess began to usurp the place once held by the god. It is possible that this was due to Babylonian and Assyrian influence. At any rate, whereas it is Sutekh who appears at the head of the Hittite states in the treaty with Ramses, in later days the chief cult of the ' Holy Cities' was paid to the Mother-goddess. His place was taken by the goddess at Carchemish as well as at Mabog, at Boghaz Keui as well as at Komana.

In the Kappadokian Komana the goddess went under the name of Ma. She was served by 6000 priests and priestesses, the whole city being dedicated to her service. The place of the king was occupied by the Abakles or high-priest. We have seen that the sculptures of Boghaz Keui give us reason to believe that the same was also the case in Pteria; we know that it was so in other 'Holy Cities' of Asia Minor. At Pessinus in Phrygia, where lions and panthers stood beside the goddess, the whole city was given up to her worship, under the command of the chief Gallos or priest ; and on the shores of the Black Sea the Amazonian priestesses of Kybele, who danced in armour in her honour, were imagined by the Greeks to constitute the sole population of an entire country. At Ephesos, in spite of the Greek colony which had found its way there, the worship of the Mother-goddess continued to absorb the life of the inhabitants, so that it still could be described in the time of St. Paul as a city which was 'a worshipper of the great goddess.' Here, as at Pessinus, she was worshipped under the form of a meteoric stone 'which had fallen from heaven.'

We may regard these ' Holy Cities,' placed under the protection of a goddess and wholly devoted to her wor-ship, as peculiarly characteristic of the Hittite race. Their two southern capitals, Kadesh and Carchemish, were cities of this kind, and their stronghold at Boghaz Keui was presumably also a consecrated place. Their progress through Asia Minor was characterised by the rise of priestly cities and the growth of a class of armed priestesses. Komana in Kappadokia, and Ephesos on the shores of the Ægean, are typical examples of such holy towns. The entire population ministered to the divinity to whom the city was dedicated, the sanctuary of the deity stood in its centre, and the chief authority was wielded by a high-priest. If a king existed by the side of the priest, he came in course of time to fill a merely subordinate position.

These 'Holy Cities' were also ' Asyla' or Cities of Refuge. The homicide could escape to them, and be

H

safe from his pursuers. Once within the precincts of the city and the protection of its deity, he could not be injured or slain. But it was not only the man who had slain another by accident who could thus claim an 'asylum' from his enemies. The debtor and the political refugee were equally safe. Doubtless the right of asylum was frequently abused, and real criminals took advantage of regulations which were intended to protect the unfortunate in an age of lawlessness and revenge. But the institution on the whole worked well, and, while it strengthened the power of the priesthood, it curbed injustice and restrained violence.

Now the institution of Cities of Refuge did not exist only in Asia Minor and in the region occupied by the Hittites. It existed also in Palestine, and it seems not unlikely that it was adopted by the great Hebrew lawgiver, acting under divine guidance, from the older population of the country. The Hebrew cities of refuge were six in number. One of them was 'Kedesh in Galilee,' whose very name declares it to have been a 'Holy City,' like Kadesh on the Orontes, while another was the ancient sanctuary of Hebron, once occupied by Hittites and Amorites. Shechem, the third city of refuge on the western side of the Jordan, had been taken by Jacob 'out of the hand of the Amorite' (Gen. xlviii. 22); and the other three cities were all on the eastern side of the Jordan, in the region so long held by Amorite tribes. We are therefore tempted to ask whether these cities had not already been 'asyla' or cities of refuge long before Moses was enjoined by God to make them such for the Israelitish conquerors of Palestine.

Closely connected with Hittite religion was Hittite art. Religion and art have been often intertwined together in the history of the world, and we can often infer the religion of a people from its art, as in the case of the sculptures of Boghaz Keui. Hittite art was a modification of that of Babylonia, and bears testimony to the same Babylonian influence as the worship of the ' Mother-goddess.' The same Chaldæan culture is presupposed by both.

But while the art of the Hittites was essentially Babylonian in origin, it was profoundly modified in the hands of the Hittite artists. The deities, indeed, were made to ride on the backs of animals, as upon Babylonian cylinders, the walls of the palaces were adorned with long rows of bas-reliefs, as in Chaldæa and Assyria, and there was the same tendency to arrange animals face to face in heraldic style ; but nevertheless the workmanship and the details introduced into it were purely native. Even a symbol like the winged solar disk assumes in Hittite sculpture a special character which can never be mistaken. The Hittite artist excelled in the representation of animal forms, but the lion, which he seems to have never wearied of designing, is treated in a peculiar way which marks it sharply off from the sculptured lions either of Babylonia or of any other country. So, too, in the case of the human figure, though the general conception has been derived from Babylonian art, the conception is worked out in a new and original manner. Those who have once seen the sculptured image of a Hittite warrior or a Hittite god, can never confuse it with the artistic productions of another race. The figure is clearly drawn from the daily experience of the sculptor's own life. The dress with its peaked shoes, the thick rounded form, the strange protrusive profile, were copied from the costume

and appearance of his fellow-countrymen, and the striking
agreement that exists between his representation of them
and that which we find on the Egyptian monuments
proves how faithfully he must have worked. The elements, in short, of Babylonian art are present in the art
of the Hittite, but the treatment and selection are his
own.

It is in his selection and combination of these elements
that he exhibits most clearly his originality. Monsters,
half human, half bestial, were known to the Babylonians,
but it was left to the Hittite to invent a double-headed
eagle, or to plant a human head on a column of lions.
The so-called rope-pattern occurs once or twice on
Babylonian gems, but it became a distinguishing characteristic of Hittite art, like the employment of the
heads only of animals instead of their entire forms.

So, again, the heraldic arrangement of animals face
to face, or more rarely back to back, had its first home
in Chaldæa, but it was the Hittites who raised it into
a principle of art. We may perhaps trace their doing
so to their love of animal forms.

The influence of Babylonian culture may have made
itself first felt in the age of the eighteenth Egyptian
dynasty, when the cuneiform tablets of Tel el-Amarna
represent the Hittite tribes as descending southward into
the Syrian plains. It may on the other hand go back to
a much earlier epoch. We have no materials at present
for deciding the question. One fact, however, is clear ;
there was a time when the Hittites were profoundly
affected by Babylonian civilisation, religion and art.
Before this could have been the case they must have
been already settled in Syria.

It is more easy to fix the period when the Hittite

sculptor received that inspiration from Egyptian art which produced the sphinxes of Eyuk and the seated image on Mount Sipylos. It can only have been the age of Ramses II., and of the great wars between Egypt and the Hittite princes in the fourteenth century before our era. The influence of Egypt was but transitory, but it was to it, in all probability, that the Hittites owed the idea of hieroglyphic writing.

At a far later date Babylonian influence was superseded by that of Assyria. The later sculptures of Carchemish betray the existence of Assyrian rather than of Babylonian models. The winged figure of the goddess of Carchemish now in the British Museum is Assyrian in style and character, and it is possible that other draped images of the goddess may be derived from the same source. In Babylonian art Istar was represented nude.

However this may be, Professor Perrot has made it clear that the beginnings of Hittite art must be looked for in Syria, on the southern slopes of the Taurus, from whence it spread to the tribes of Kappadokia. It is in Northern Syria that its rudest and most infantile attempts have been found. The sculptors of Eyuk were already advanced in skill.

To Professor Perrot we also owe the discovery of bronze figures of Hittite manufacture. The execution of them is at once conventional and barbarous. Nothing can exceed the rudeness of a figure now in the Louvre, which represents a god with a pointed tiara, standing on the back of an animal. Though the face of the god has evidently been modelled with care, it is impossible to tell to what zoological species the animal which supports him is intended to belong. Almost equally far removed from nature is the bronze image of a bull which is also in the Louvre.

If these bronzes are to be regarded as the highest efforts of Hittite metallurgic work, it is not to be regretted that they are few in number. But it is quite different with the engraved gems which we now know to have been of Hittite workmanship. Many of them are exceedingly fine ; a hæmatite cylinder, for instance, which was discovered at Kappadokia, is equal to the best products of Babylonian art. The gems and cylinders were for the most part intended to be used as seals, and some of them are provided with handles cut out of the stone, the seal itself having designs on four, and sometimes on five faces. These handles seem to be a peculiarity of Hittite art, or at least of the art which derived its inspiration from that of the Hittites. Another peculiarity noticeable in many of the gems, consists in enclosing the inner field of the engraved design with one or more concentric circles, each circle containing an elaborate series of ornaments or figures, or even characters, though the characters are usually placed in the central field. Thus two gems have been found at Yuzghat, in Kappadokia, so much alike, that they must have been the work of the same artist. On the larger an inscription has been engraved in the centre, round which runs a circle containing a large number of beautifully-executed figures. The winged solar disk rests upon the symbol of ' kingship,' on either side of which kneels a figure, half man and half bull. On the right and left is the figure of a standing priest, behind whom we see on the left a man adoring what seems to be the stump of a tree, while on the right are a tree, two arrows and a quiver, a basket, a stag's head, and a seated deity, above whose hand is a bird. The two groups are separated by the picture of a boot—the symbol, it may be, of the earth—which rests, like the winged solar disk, on the symbol of royalty. The smaller seal has a different inscription in the centre, encircled by two rings, one containing a row of ornaments, and the other the same figures as those engraved on the larger seal, excepting only that the arrangement of the figures has been changed, and a tree introduced among them. What is curious, however, is that a gem has been found at Aidin, far away towards the western extremity of Asia Minor, containing a central inscription almost identical with that of the smaller Yuzghat seal, though the figures which surround it are not the same.

These circular seals must be regarded not only as characteristic of Hittite art, but also as a product of Hittite invention. We meet with nothing resembling them in Babylonia or Assyria.

The gems can be traced across the Ægean to the shores of Greece. Among the objects discovered by Dr. Schliemann at Mykenæ were two rings of gold, on the chatons of which designs are engraved in what we may now recognise as the Hittite style of art. On one of them are two rows of animals' heads ; on the other an elaborate picture, which reminds us of the elaborate designs on the gems of Asia Minor. It represents a woman under a tree, facing two other persons, who wear the upturned boots and flounced dress that we find in Hittite sculptures, while the background is filled in with the heads of animals.

These gems are not the only indication the ruins of Mykenæ have afforded that Hittite influence was spread beyond the coasts of Asia Minor. Allusion has already been made to the figures of the Hittite goddess and the doves that rested on the pinnacles of her temple ; another figure in thin gold gives us a likeness of the Hittite goddess seated on the cliff of Sipylos, as she appeared before rain and tempest had changed her into 'the weeping Niobe.' Perhaps, however, the most striking illustration of the westward migration of Hittite influence, is to be found in the famous lions which stand fronting each other, carved on stone, above the great gate of the ancient Peloponnesian city. The lions of Mykenæ have long been known as the oldest piece of sculpture in Europe, but the art which inspired it was of Hittite origin. A similar bas-relief has been discovered at Kümbet, in Phrygia, in the near vicinity of Hittite monuments ; and we have just seen that the heraldic position in which the lions are represented was a peculiar feature of Hittite art.

Greek tradition affirmed that the rulers of Mykenæ had come from Lydia, bringing with them the civilisation and the treasures of Asia Minor. The tradition has been confirmed by modern research. While certain elements belonging to the prehistoric culture of Greece, as revealed at Mykenæ and elsewhere, were derived from Egypt and Phœnicia, there are others which point to Asia Minor as their source. And the culture of Asia Minor was Hittite. Mr. Gladstone, therefore, may be right in seeing the Hittites in the Keteians of Homer—that Homer who told of the legendary glories of Mykenæ and the Lydian dynasty which held it in possession. Even the buckle, with the help of which the prehistoric Greek fastened his cloak, has been shown by a German scholar to imply an arrangement of the dress such as we see represented on the Hittite monument of Ibreez.

For us of the modern world, therefore, the resurrection of the Hittite people from their long sleep of oblivion possesses a double interest. They appeal to us not alone because of the influence they once exercised on the fortunes of the Chosen People, not alone because a Hittite was the wife of David and the ancestress of Christ, but also on account of the debt which the civilisation of our own Europe owes to them. Our culture is the inheritance we have received from ancient Greece, and the first beginnings of Greek culture were derived from the Hittite conquerors of Asia Minor. The Hittite warriors who still guard the Pass of Karabel, on the very threshold of Asia, are symbols of the position occupied by the race in the education of mankind. The Hittites carried the time-worn civilisations of Babylonia and Egypt to the furthest boundary of Asia, and there handed them over to the West in the grey dawn of European history. But they never passed the boundary themselves ; with the conquest of Lydia their mission was accomplished, the work that had been appointed them was fulfilled.

AN INSCRIPTION FOUND AT CARCHEMISH (*now destroyed*).

CHAPTER VII.

THE INSCRIPTIONS.

HOW can the history of a lost people be recovered, it may be asked, except through the help of the records they have left behind them? How can we come to know anything about the Hittites until their few and fragmentary inscriptions are deciphered? The answer to this question will have been furnished by the preceding pages. Though the Hittite inscriptions are still undeciphered, though the number of them is still very small, there are other materials for reconstructing the history of the race, and these materials have now found their interpreter. The sculptured monuments the Hittites have left behind them, the seals they engraved, the cities they inhabited, the memorials of them preserved in the Old Testament, in the cuneiform tablets of Assyria, and in the papyri of Egypt, have all served to build up afresh the fabric of a mighty empire which once exercised so profound an influence on the destinies of the civilised world.

But the Hittite inscriptions have not been altogether useless. They have helped to connect together the scattered monuments of Hittite dominion, and to prove that the peculiar art they display was of Hittite origin. It was the Hittite hieroglyphs which accompany the figure of the warrior in the Pass of Karabel, and of the sitting goddess on Mount Sipylos, that proved these sculptures to be of Hittite origin. It has similarly been inscriptions containing Hittite characters which have enabled us to trace the march of the Hittite armies along the high-roads of Asia Minor, and to feel sure that Hittite princes once reigned in the city of Hamath.

The Hittite texts are distinguished by two characteristics. With hardly an exception, the hieroglyphs that compose them are carved in relief instead of being incised, and the lines read alternately from right to left and from left to right. The direction in which the characters look determines the direction in which they should be read. This alternate or *boustrophedon* mode of writing also characterises early Greek inscriptions, and since it was not adopted by either Phœnicians, Egyptians, or Assyrians, the question arises whether the Greeks did not learn to write in such a fashion from neighbours who made use of the Hittite script.

Another characteristic of Hittite writing is the frequent employment of the heads of animals and men.

It is very rarely that the whole body of an animal is drawn ; the head alone was considered sufficient. This peculiarity would of itself mark off the Hittite hiero-glyphs from those of Egypt.

But a very short inspection of the characters is enough to show that the Hittites could not have borrowed them from the Egyptians. The two forms of writing are ut-terly and entirely distinct. Two of the most common Hittite characters represent the snow-boot and the fingerless glove, which, as we have seen, indicate the northern ancestry of the Hittite tribes, while the ideo-graph which denotes a 'country' is a picture of the mountain peaks of the Kappadokian plateau. It would therefore seem that the system of writing was invented in Kappadokia, and not in the southern regions of Syria or Canaan.

We may gather, however, that the invention took place after the contact of the Hittites with Egypt, and their consequent acquaintance with the Egyptian form of script. Similar occurrences have happened in modern times. A Cheroki Indian in North America, who had seen the books of the white man, was led thereby to devise an elaborate mode of writing for his own country-men, and the curious syllabary invented for the Vei negroes by one of their tribe originated in the same manner. So, too, we may imagine that the sight of the hieroglyphs of Egypt, and the knowledge that thoughts could be conveyed by them, suggested to some Hittite genius the idea of inventing a similar means of inter-communication for his own people.

At any rate, it is pretty clear that the Hittite charac-ters are used like the Egyptian, sometimes as ideographs to express ideas, sometimes phonetically to represent syllables and sounds, sometimes as determinatives to denote the class to which the word belongs to which they are attached. It is probable, moreover, that a word or sound was often expressed by multiplying the characters which expressed the whole or part of it, just as was the case in Egyptian writing in the age of Ramses II. At the same time the number of separate characters used by the Hittites was far less than that employed by the Egyptian scribes. At present not 200 are known to exist, though almost every fresh inscription adds to the list.

The oldest writing material of the Hittites were their plates of metal, on the surface of which the characters were hammered out from behind. The Hittite copy of the treaty with Ramses II. was engraved in this manner on a plate of silver, its centre being occupied with a representation of the god Sutekh embracing the Hittite king, and a short line of hieroglyphs running round him. This central ornamentation, surrounded with a circular band of figures, was in accordance with the usual style of Hittite art. The Egyptian monuments show us what the silver plate was like. It was of rectangular shape, with a ring at the top by which it could be suspended from the wall. If ever the tomb of Ur-Maa Noferu-Ra, the Hittite wife of Ramses, is discovered, it is possible that a Hittite copy of the famous treaty may be found among its contents.

At all events, it is clear that already at this period the Hittites were a literary people. The Egyptian records make mention of a certain Khilip-sira, whose name is compounded with that of Khilip or Aleppo, and describe him as 'a writer of books of the vile Kheta.' Like the Egyptian Pharaoh, the Hittite monarch was

accompanied to battle by his scribes.   If Kirjath-sepher
or 'Book-town,' in the neighbourhood of Hebron, was
of Hittite origin, the Hittites would have possessed
libraries like the Assyrians, which may yet be dug up.
Kirjath-sepher was also called Debir, 'the sanctuary,'
and we may therefore conclude that the library was
stored in its chief temple, as were the libraries of Babylonia.   There was another Debir or Dapur further north,
in the vicinity of Kadesh on the Orontes, which is mentioned in the Egyptian inscriptions ; and since this was
in the land of the Amorites, while Kirjath-sepher is
also described as an Amorite town, it is possible that
here too the relics of an ancient library may yet be
found.   We must not forget that in the days of Deborah,
'out of Zebulon,' northward of Megiddo, came 'they
that handle the pen of the writer' (Judg. v. 14).

The inscriptions recently discovered at Tel el-Amarna
in Egypt have shown that in the century before the
Exodus the common medium of literary intercourse in
Western Asia was the language and cuneiform script of
Babylonia.   It was subsequently to this that the Hittites
forced their way southward, bringing with them their
own peculiar system of hieroglyphic writing.   But the
cuneiform characters still continued to be used in the
Hittite region of the world.   Cuneiform tablets have
been purchased at Kaisarîyeh which come from some
old library of Kappadokia, the site of which is still unknown, and Dr. Humann has lately discovered a long
cuneiform inscription among the Hittite sculptures of
Sinjirli in the ancient Komagene.   If the Hittite texts
are ever deciphered, it will probably be through the help
of the cuneiform script.

A beginning has already been made.   Within a month

after my Paper had been read before the Society of
Biblical Archæology, which announced the discovery
of a Hittite empire and the connection of the curious
art of Asia Minor with that of Carchemish, I had fallen
across a bilingual inscription in Hittite and cuneiform
characters. This was on the silver boss of King Tarkondemos, the only key yet found to the interpretation
of the Hittite texts.

THE BILINGUAL BOSS OF TARKONDEMOS.

The story of the boss is a strange one. It was purchased many years ago at Smyrna by M. Alexander
Jovanoff, a well-known numismatist of Constantinople,
who showed it to the Oriental scholar Dr. A. D. Mordtmann. Dr. Mordtmann made a copy of it, and found it
to be a round silver plate, probably the head of a dagger
or dirk, round the rim of which ran a cuneiform inscription. Within, occupying the central field, was the figure
of a warrior in a new and unknown style of art. He
stood erect, holding a spear in the right hand, and
pressing the left against his breast. He was clothed
in a tunic, over which a fringed cloak was thrown ; a

close-fitting cap was on the head, and boots with upturned ends on the feet, the upper part of the legs being
bare, while a dirk was fastened in the belt. On either
side of the figure was a series of 'symbols,' the series
on each side being the same, except that on the right
side the upper 'symbols' were smaller, and the lower
'symbols' larger than the corresponding ones on the
left side.

In an article published some years later on the cuneiform inscriptions of Van, Dr. Mordtmann referred to the
boss, and it was his description of the figure in the
centre of it which arrested my attention. I saw at once
that the figure must be in the style of art I had just
determined to be Hittite, and I guessed that the 'symbols' which accompanied it would turn out to be Hittite
hieroglyphs. Dr. Mordtmann stated that he had given
a copy of the boss in 1862 in the 'Numismatic Journal
which appears in Hanover.' After a long and trouble-
some search I found that the publication meant by him
was not a Journal at all, and had appeared at Leipzig,
not at Hanover, in 1863, not in 1862. The copy of the
boss contained in it showed that I was right in believing
. Dr. Mordtmann's 'symbols' to be Hittite characters.

It now became necessary to know how far the copy
was correct, and to ascertain whether the original were
still in existence. A reply soon came from the British
Museum. The boss had once been offered to the
Museum for sale, but rejected, as nothing like it had
ever been seen before, and it was therefore suspected
of being a forgery. Before its rejection, however, an
electrotype had been taken of it, an impression of which
was now sent to me.

Shortly afterwards came another communication from

M. François Lenormant, one of the most learned and brilliant Oriental scholars of the present century. He had seen the original at Constantinople some twenty years previously, and had there made a cast of it, which he forwarded to me. The cast and the electrotype agreed exactly together.

There could accordingly be no doubt that we had before us, if not the original itself, a perfect facsimile of it. The importance of this fact soon became manifest, for the original boss disappeared after M. Jovanoff's death, and in spite of all enquiries no trace of it can be discovered. It may be recovered hereafter in the bazaars of Constantinople or in some private house at St. Petersburg ; at present there is no clue whatever to its actual possessor.

The reading of the cuneiform legend offers but little difficulty. It gives us the name and title of the king whose figure is engraved within it—' Tarqu-dimme king of the country of Erme.'

The name Tarqu-dimme is evidently the same as that of the Cilician prince Tarkondemos or Tarkondimotos, who lived in the time of our Lord. The name is also met with in other parts of Asia Minor under the forms of Tarkondas and Tarkondimatos ; and we may consider it to be of a distinctively Hittite type. Where the district was over which Tarqu-dimme ruled we can only guess. It may have been the range of mountains called Arima by the classical writers, which lay close under the Hittite monuments of the Bulgar Dagh. In this case Tarkondemos would have been a Cilician king.

The twice-repeated Hittite version of the cuneiform legend has been the subject of much discussion. The

I

arrangement of the characters, due more to the necessity
of filling up the vacant space on the boss than to the
requirements of their natural order, allowed more than
one interpretation of them.   But there were two facts
which furnished the key to their true reading.   On
the one hand, the inscription is divided into two halves
by two characters whose form and position in other
Hittite texts show them to signify 'king' and 'country';
on the other hand, the first two characters are made,
as it were, to issue from the mouth of the king, and
thus to express his name.   We thus obtain the reading:
'Tarku-dimme king of the country of Er-me,' the
syllables *tarku* and *me* being denoted by the head of
a goat and the numeral 'four,' while the ideographs
of 'king' and 'country' are represented by the royal
tiara worn by gods and monarchs in the Hittite sculptures, and by the picture of a mountainous land.   In
the ideograph of 'country' Mordtmann had already
seen a likeness of the shafts of rock which rise out of
the Kappadokian plateau.

The bilingual boss accordingly furnishes us with two
important ideographs, and the phonetic values of four
other characters.   Armed with these, we can attack
the other texts, and learn something about them.   It
becomes clear that the inscriptions from Carchemish
now in the British Museum are the monuments of a
king whose name ends in -me-Tarku, and who records
the names of his father and grandfather.   To the grandfather belonged an inscription copied by Mr. Boscawen
among the ruins of Carchemish, but unfortunately
never brought to England, and probably long since
destroyed.

On the lion of Merash, moreover, a king similarly

records his name along with those of his two immediate ancestors. The same king's name is found at Hamath as that of the father of the sovereign mentioned in the other inscriptions that come from there, and we may perhaps infer that the monuments of Hamath are the memorials of a Komagenian monarch who carried his victorious arms thus far to the south. The

THE LION OF MERASH.

time will doubtless come when we shall be able to read these mysterious characters without difficulty, and we shall then know whether or not our inference is correct.

Meanwhile we must be content to await the discovery of another bilingual text. The legend on the boss of Tarkondemos is not long enough to carry us far through the mazes of Hittite decipherment ; before much progress can be made it must be supplemented by another inscription of the same kind. But the fact that one bilingual inscription has been found is an earnest that other bilingual inscriptions have existed, and may yet be brought to light. We may live in confident expectation that the mute stones will yet be taught to speak, and that we shall learn how the empire of the Hittites was founded and preserved, not from the annals of their enemies, but from their own lips.

It is not probable that the Hittite system of writing passed away without leaving its influence behind it. As the culture and art which the Hittites carried to the barbarous nations of Asia Minor became implanted among them and bore abundant fruit, so too we may believe that the knowledge of the Hittite writing did not perish utterly. There is reason to think that the curious syllabary which continued to be used in Cyprus as late as the age of Alexander the Great was derived from the Hittite hieroglyphs. It was singularly un-fitted to express the sounds of the Greek language, as it was required to do in Cyprus, and it has been shown that it was but a branch of a syllabary once employed throughout a large part of Asia Minor, the very country in which the Hittites engraved their own written monuments. It seems likely, therefore, that the Hittite characters became a syllabary in which each character represented a separate syllable, and survived in this form to a late age.

It is also possible that the names assigned to the letters even of the Phœnician alphabet were influ-enced by the hieroglyphs of the Hittites. When the Phœnicians borrowed the letters of the Egyptian alphabet they gave them names beginning in their own language with the sound represented by each letter. *A* was called *aleph* because the Phœnician word *aleph* 'an ox' began with that sound, *k* was *kaph* 'the hand' because *kaph* in Phœnician began with *k*. It was but an early application of the same principle which made our forefathers believe that the child would learn his alphabet more quickly if he was taught that '*A* was an archer who shot at a frog.'

But the names must have been assigned to the letters not only because they commenced with corresponding sounds, but also because of their fancied resemblance to the objects denoted by the names. Now in some instances the resemblance is by no means clear. The earliest forms of the letters called *kaph* and *yod*, for example, both of which words signify a 'hand,' have little likeness to the human hand. If we turn to the Hittite hieroglyphs, however, we find among them two representations of the hand, encased in the long Hittite glove, which are almost identical with the Phœnician letters in shape. It is difficult, therefore, to resist the conviction that the letters *kaph* and *yod* received their names from Syrians who were familiar with the appearance of the Hittite characters. It is the same in the case of *aleph*. Here too the old Phœnician letter does not in any way resemble an ox, but it bears a very close likeness to the head of a bull, which occupies a prominent place in the Hittite texts. *Aleph* became the Greek *alpha* when the Phœnician alphabet was handed on to the Greeks, and in the word *alphabet* has become part of our own heritage. Like *yod*, which has passed through the Greek *iota* into the English *jot*, it is thus possible that there are still words in daily use among ourselves which

can be traced, if not to the Hittite language, at all
events to the Hittite script.

What the language of the Hittites was we have yet
to learn.   But the proper names preserved on the
Egyptian and Assyrian monuments show that it did not
belong to the Semitic family of speech, and an analysis
of the Hittite inscriptions further makes it evident that
it made large use of suffixes.   But we must be on our
guard against supposing that the language was uniform
throughout the district in which the Hittite population
lived.   Different tribes doubtless spoke different dialects,
and some of these dialects probably differed widely from
each other.   But they all belonged to the same general
type and class of language, and may therefore be collectively spoken of as the Hittite language, just as the
various dialects of England are collectively termed
English.   Indeed, we find the same type of language
extending far eastward of Kappadokia, if we may trust
the proper names recorded in the Assyrian inscriptions.
Names of a distinctively Hittite cast are met with as far
as the frontiers of the ancient kingdom of Ararat, and it
may be that the language of Ararat itself, the so-called
Vannic, may belong to the same family of speech.   As
the cuneiform inscriptions in which this language is
embodied have now been deciphered, we shall be able
to determine the question as soon as the Hittite texts
also render up their secrets.

In the south of Palestine the Hittites must have lost
their old language and have adopted that of their
Semitic neighbours at an early period.   In Northern
Syria the change was longer in coming about.   The
last king of Carchemish bears a non-Semitic name, but
a Semitic god was worshipped at Aleppo, and Kadesh

on the Orontes remained a Semitic sanctuary. The Hittite occupation of Hamath seems to have lasted for a short time only. Its king, who appears on the Assyrian monuments as the contemporary of Ahab, has the Semitic name of Irkhulena, 'the moon-god belongs to us'; and his successors were equally of Semitic origin. It is more doubtful whether Tou or Toi, whose son came to David with an offer of alliance, bears a name which can be explained from the Semitic lexicon.

In the fastnesses of the Taurus, however, the Hittite dialects were slow in dying. In the days of St. Paul the people of Lystra still spoke 'the speech of Lykaonia,' although the official language of Kappadokia had long since become Aramaic. But the Aramaic was itself supplanted by Greek, and before the downfall of the Roman empire Greek was the common language of all Asia Minor. In its turn Greek has been superseded in these modern times by Turkish.

Languages, however, may change and perish, but the races that have spoken them remain. The characteristics of race, once acquired, are slow to alter. Though the last echoes of Hittite speech have died away centuries ago, the Hittite race still inhabits the region from which in ancient days it poured down upon the cities of the south. We may still see in it all the lineaments of the warriors of Karabel or the sculptured princes of Carchemish; even the snow-shoe and fingerless glove are still worn on the cold uplands of Kappadokia.

CHAPTER VIII.

HITTITE TRADE AND INDUSTRY.

THE Hittites shone as much in the arts of peace as in the arts of war. The very fact that they invented a system of writing speaks highly for their intellectual capacities. It has been granted to but few among the races of mankind to devise means of communicating their thoughts otherwise than by words; most of the nations of the world have been content to borrow from others not only the written characters they use but even the conception of writing itself.

We know from the ruins of Boghaz Keui and Eyuk that the Hittites were no mean architects. They understood thoroughly the art of fortification; the great moat outside the walls of Boghaz Keui, with its sides of slippery stone, is a masterpiece in this respect, like the fortified citadels within the city, to which the besieged could retire when the outer wall was captured. The well-cut blocks and sculptured slabs of which their palaces were built prove how well they knew the art of quarrying and fashioning stone. The mines of the Bulgar Dagh are an equally clear indication of their skill in mining and metallurgic work.

The metallurgic fame of the Khalybes, who bordered on the Hittite territory, and may have belonged to the same race, was spread through the Greek world. They had the reputation of first discovering how to harden iron into steel. It was from them, at all events, that the Greeks acquired the art.

Silver and copper appear, from the evidence of the Egyptian and Assyrian monuments, to have been the metals most in request, though gold and iron also figure among the objects which the Hittites offered in tribute. The gold and copper were moulded into cups and images of animals, and the copper was changed into bronze by being mixed with tin. From whence the tin was procured we have yet to learn.

Silver and iron were alike used as a medium of exchange. The Assyrian king received from Carchemish 250 talents of iron ; and the excavations of Dr. Schliemann among the ruins of Troy have afforded evidence that silver also was employed by the Hittites in place of money, and that its use for this purpose was communicated by them to the most distant nations of Western Asia Minor.

In the so-called 'treasure of Priam,' disinterred among the calcined ruins of Hissarlik or Troy, are six blade-like ingots of silver, about seven or eight inches in length and two in breadth. Mr. Barclay Head has pointed out that each of these ingots weighs the third part of a Babylonian maneh or mina, and further that this particular maneh of 8656 grains Troy, was once employed throughout Asia Minor for weighing bullion silver. It differed from the standard of weight and value used in Phœnicia, Assyria, and Asia Minor itself in the later Greek age. But it corresponded with 'the maneh of Carchemish' mentioned in the Assyrian contract tablets, which continued to hold its own even after the conquest of Carchemish by Sargon. The maneh of

Carchemish had, it is true, been originally derived from Babylonia, like most of the elements of Hittite culture, but it had made itself so thoroughly at home in the Hittite capital as to be called after its name. Nothing can show more clearly than this the leading position held by the Hittites in general, and the city of Carchemish in particular, in regard to commerce and industry.

Carchemish was, in fact, the centre of the overland trade in Western Asia. It commanded the high-road which brought the products of Phœnicia and the West to the civilised populations of Assyria and Babylon. It was this which made its possession so greatly coveted by the Assyrian kings. Its capture assured to Sargon the command of the Mediterranean coast, and the transference to Assyrian hands of the commerce and wealth which had flowed in to the merchant-princes of the Hittite city.

The sumptuous furniture in which they indulged is mentioned by Assur-natsir-pal. Like the luxurious monarchs of Israel, they reclined on couches inlaid with ivory, of which it is possible that they were the inventors. At all events, elephants were still hunted by Tiglath-pileser I., in the neighbourhood of Carchemish, as they had been by Thothmes III. four centuries earlier, and elephants' tusks were among the tribute paid by the Hittites to the Assyrian kings. It may be that the extinction of the elephant in this part of Asia was due to Hittite huntsmen.

The ivory couches of Carchemish, however, were not employed at meals, as they would have been in Assyria or among the Greeks and Romans of a later day. Like the Egyptians, the Hittites sat when eating, and their chairs were provided with backs as well as with curiously-formed footstools. The food was placed on low cross-legged tables, which resembled a camp-stool in shape.

At times, as we may gather from a bas-relief at Merash, they entertained themselves at a banquet with the sounds of music. Several different kinds of musical instruments are represented on the monuments, among which we may recognise a lyre, a trumpet, and a sort of guitar. It is evident that they were fond of music, and had cultivated the art, as befitted a people to whom wealth had given leisure. A curious indication of the same leisured ease is to be found in a sculpture at Eyuk, where an attendant is depicted carrying a monkey on his shoulders. Those only who enjoyed the quiet of a peaceful and wealthy life would have gratified the taste for animals which the monuments reveal, by importing an animal like the monkey from the distant south. The Hittites were doubtless a warlike people when they first swooped down upon the plains of Syria, but they soon began to cultivate the arts of peace and to become one of the great mercantile peoples of the ancient world.

We learn from the Books of Kings that horses and chariots were exported from Egypt for the Hittite princes, the Israelites serving as intermediaries in the trade. But they must also have obtained horses from the north, and perhaps have bred them for themselves. The prophet Ezekiel tells us (xxvii. 14) that 'they of Togarmah traded' in the fairs of Tyre 'with horses and horsemen and mules,' and Togarmah has been identified with the Tul-Garimmi of the Assyrian inscriptions, which was situated in Komagene. In the wars between Egypt and Kadesh a portion of the Hittite army fought in chariots, each drawn by two horses, and holding sometimes two, sometimes three men. The chariots

were of light make, and rested on two wheels, usually
furnished with six spokes.

The army was well-disciplined and well-arranged. Its
nucleus was formed of native-born Hittites, who occupied
the centre and the posts of danger. Around them were
ranged their allies and mercenaries, under the command
of special generals. The native infantry and cavalry
also obeyed separate captains, but the whole host was
led by a single commander-in-chief.

We have yet to be made acquainted with the details
of their domestic architecture. The ground-plan of their
palaces has been given us at Boghaz Keui and Eyuk, at
Carchemish and Sinjirli, and we know that they were built
round a central court of quadrangular form. We know
too that the entrance to the palace was, like that to an
Egyptian temple, flanked by massive blocks of stone on
either side, and approached by an avenue of sculptured
slabs. We have learned, moreover, that the palace was
erected on raised terraces or mounds ; but beyond this
we know little except that use was made of a pillar
without a base, which had been originally derived from
Babylonia, the primitive home of columnar architecture.

About the Hittite dress we have fuller information.
Apart from the snow-shoes or mocassins which have
helped to identify their monumental remains, we have
found the Hittites wearing on their heads two kinds of
covering, one a close-fitting skull-cap, the other a lofty
tiara, generally pointed, but sometimes rounded at the
top or ornamented, as at Ibreez, with horn-like ribbons.
The pointed tiara was adorned with perpendicular lines
of embroidery. At Boghaz Keui the goddesses have
what has been termed the mural crown, resembling as it
does the fortified wall of a town.

The robes of the women descended to the feet. This was also the case with the long sleeved garment of the priests, but other men wore a tunic which left the knees bare, and was fastened round the waist by a girdle. Over this was thrown a cloak, which in walking left one leg exposed. In the girdle was stuck a short dirk ; the other arms carried being a spear and a bow, which was slung behind the back. The double-headed battle-axe was also a distinctively Hittite weapon, and was carried by them to the coast of the Ægean, where in the Greek age it became the symbol of the Karian Zeus, and of the island of Tenedos. All these weapons were of bronze, or perhaps of iron ; but there are indications that the Hittite tribes had once contented themselves with tools and weapons of stone. Near the site of Arpad Mr. Boscawen purchased a large and beautiful axe-head of highly polished green-stone, which could, however, never have been intended for actual use. It was, in fact, a sacrificial weapon, surviving in the service of the gods from the days when the working of metal was not yet known. Like other survivals in religious worship, it bore witness to a social condition that had long since passed away. A small axe-head, also of polished green-stone, was obtained by myself from the neighbourhood of Ephesos, and bears a remarkable resemblance in form to the axe-head of Arpad. The importance of this fact becomes manifest when we compare the numerous other weapons or implements of polished stone found in Western Asia Minor, which exhibit quite a different shape. It permits the conclusion that both Arpad and Ephesos were seats of Hittite influence, and that in both the same form of stone implement—a survival from an earlier age of stone—was dedicated to the service of the gods.

The dresses of cloth and linen with which the Hittites clothed themselves were dyed with various colours, and were ornamented with fringes and rich designs. That of the priest at Ibreez is especially worthy of study. Among the patterns with which it is adorned are the same square ornament as is met with on the tomb of the Phrygian king Midas, and the curious symbol usually known as the 'swastika,' which has become so famous since the excavations of General di Cesnola in Cyprus, and of Dr. Schliemann at Troy. The symbol recurs times without number on the pre-historic pottery of Cyprus and the Trojan plain ; but no trace of it has ever yet been found in Egypt, in Assyria, or in Babylonia. Alone among the remains of the civilised nations of the ancient East the rock-sculpture of Ibreez displays it on the robe of a Lykaonian priest. Was it an invention of the Hittite people, communicated by them to the rude tribes of Asia Minor, along with the other elements of a cultured life, or was it of barbarous origin, adopted by the Hittites from the earlier population of the West ?

Before we can answer this question we must know far more than we do at present about that long-forgotten but wonderful race, whose restoration to history has been one of the most curious discoveries of the present age. When the sites of the old Hittite cities have been thoroughly explored, when the monuments they left behind them have been disinterred, and their inscriptions have been deciphered and read, we shall doubtless learn the answers to this and many other questions that are now pressing for solution. Meanwhile we must be content with what has already been gained. Light has been cast upon a dark page in the history of Western Asia, and therewith upon the sacred record of the Old Testament, and a people has advanced into the forefront of modern knowledge who exercised a deep influence upon the fortunes of Israel, though hitherto they had been to us little more than a name. At the very moment when every word of Scripture is being minutely scrutinised, now by friends, now by foes, we have learnt that the statement once supposed to impugn the authority of the sacred narrative is the best witness to its truth. The friends of Abraham, the allies of David, the mother of Solomon, all belonged to a race which left an indelible mark on the history of the world, though it has been reserved in God's wisdom for our own generation to discover and trace it out.

INDEX.

———

LIST OF SCRIPTURE REFERENCES.

3528368R00091

Printed in Germany
by Amazon Distribution
GmbH, Leipzig